On the Brink of a Breakthrough!

Breakthrough!

Your Time is Now!

Kimberly R. Lee

October 2015

Table of Contents

Table of Contents

Acknowledgements

On the Brink of Breakthrough is a must read for all Believers and Non-Believers. Prophetess Kim Lee gives understanding of how to see life' s challenges in a different way and the fact that we are closer to breakthrough than we think. As people read this book, there will be numerous breakthroughs and healings in their lives.

Apostle Kevin L. Jenkins

Apostle Kevin L. Jenkins

Kevin L. Jenkins Ministries

On the Brink of a Breakthrough dares us to believe that "our purpose is bigger than our immediate circle or circumstances." Although our paths may be riddled with pain it was never designed to kill us but, if we allow it, can propel us into our purpose. The author graciously encourages and challenges us to hide God' s word in our heart while simultaneously keeping it in our mouths as the catalyst for our faith and subsequent breakthrough. We are repeatedly exhorted to take heart and believe that we will overcome with the express help of our God, if we will persevere (by doing our part) and stand on God' s word. We are consistently reminded in this ***Breakthrough Manifesto*** that God is drawn to His word and He has purposed to fulfill it. This book of hope is replete with scripture that we can add to our arsenal to fight the good fight of faith; because as the author so aptly implies - *as we align our thoughts with His thoughts, we change the very course of our lives.* I recommend this book to anyone who is tired of being tired and ready for a life change. The author truly comes along side you as a fellow sojourner sharing key information that will spur you on to your breakthrough! It's Time!

Terikka Faciane, M.Ed.

Author of the book *The Journey towards Transformative Leadership*

www.itstimeinc.com

Prophetess Kimberly Lee,

Please find the book review. It is awesome, thoroughly enjoyed it!!

"On the Brink of a Breakthrough" is a profound masterpiece for breakthroughs. It's empowering, enlightening as well as, filled with relevant practical applications. Everyone that reads it will be tremendously blessed! Blessings!

Graciously,

Dr. Helen Orme
Senior Pastor at Shekinah Glory Tabernacle
Renton, Washington

On the Brink of a Breakthrough!

Breakthrough:

A sudden advance, especially in knowledge or technique; an act or instance of breaking through an obstacle. An offensive thrust that penetrates and carries beyond a defensive line in warfare.

Exasperated with foolishness? Done feeling like you are beating the air to utter exhaustion and missing the target every time? Feel like you are surrounded by an ambush and about to be pounced on by a fierce enemy? If any of this has been the case for you it means you have realized the boundaries that are holding you hostage and it is time leave excessive comfort zones and breakthrough to new heights in life! I believe, when life gets hard it is not calling for us to shrink but offering us an opportunity for God to bring the *champion* out of us. Ask yourself, why am I here? What is causing me to be or feel stuck? I can guarantee it is probably a combination of things that need to be addressed practically and spiritually. We have access to an abundant life, so what is keeping us from that abundance? Where can a shift in our thinking change everything?

What do you need to let go of in order to break through? We can always begin again and what better place to start than a board meeting with God the CEO of your soul and cast your care on God and begin fresh! The enemy of your soul knows you have purpose and is on assignment to kill, steal and destroy (John 10:10) your purpose, progress and sense of peace. Think it not strange, something will always come to test your desire for true growth and success. It is during times of testing that we must tweak our perspective from victim to victor by faith. The tests of life may send the hottest of fires that seemingly exasperate and exhaust us but there is hope in the fact that there is no furnace hot enough that the Angel of God, the Lord Jesus Christ will not walk through with you to see that your are purified for your promotion.

Have you found yourself saying, "I cannot stay in this place, I need change." Are you on autopilot in some areas of your life? I ask you another question then, where do you want to go from here? Write it down and make it plain so you can move toward what you see. A paradigm shift, a transformational way of thinking is needed to bring revolution into your life. We cannot change our actions, reactions or habits until we abandon certain ways of thinking and the actions that follow habitual boundary setting. It is likened unto being deformed in a certain way and you build your life around the deformity which gives unclear perspective. I am reminded of the woman in the Bible (Luke 13:11) who was twisted and bound for 18 years until she had an encounter with Jesus Christ. As He was teaching in the synagogue he noticed her and had compassion on her. He called the twisted and bound woman to Himself to speak a word of life to her, touch her physically with power so that she could stand up and glorify God. I believe there are certain areas in our lives where God wants to free us completely so we can see life in a new way whether it be natural or spiritual. I believe **God wants to change our perspective view from symbolically looking at life through the lenses of disability to His ability within us.** Yes, it can be uncomfortable to change our failing perspective but in the long run having a new, wealthy viewpoint will be worth the work. Scripture denotes the heart of God for us to be well, Paul the man of God says, "Beloved I pray that you would prosper in every way and that your body will keep well, even as I know your soul keeps well and prospers (3 John 1:2 Amplified). Our entire person and the quality of our lives is important to God; so our whole man flourishing (even through times of famine) is God's heart toward us.

The life changes we experience can feel excruciating and trials last so long one feels like giving up and giving in but would never confess it openly for fear of looking too frustrated and a like a failure. I can confess to wearing that mask of perfection trying to look like you have it all together but really crying inside to just cut the cord of falsity and be yourself. In addition to being yourself being courageous enough to cry out for help in the areas you're flailing about in life. Once you do take it off, God can truly help you and prune you for your best life. It's a process, yes, but in the end worth embracing. **Unmasking**

unveils you so you can truly pursue purpose in freedom. Who can you truly be real with about yourself flaws and all? If no one, then go talk to God about your inadequacy so he can talk to you about His adequacy and grace for your life. A friend told me once, she asked God, "What do I say when people ask me how long do I have to stay in the fire?" She said the Lord told her, "As long as it takes them to believe I am walking with them and start acting like it." So if this theme rings true and I believe it does, breakthrough is as much the process and it is progress. **With that train of thought we can begin our journey to breakthrough by taking time out to reflect and pray about the changes we are experiencing.** I was reminded recently of how Jesus prayed; he never rehearsed problems but he always told people things like only believe, don' t fear and then he prayed the desired result he wanted to see for those who approached Him. In Jesus' wilderness experience he was bombarded with thoughts and suggestions from the devil of how Jesus should shift (give) His authority over to the devil. That' s powerful, because the devil wants you and me to shift our authority over to him still today. Jesus kept over riding the enemy' s suggestive attempts and his own present circumstance by retorting with the Word of God until eventually the devil left him alone for a season and Jesus left the wilderness with power. In my own life, I needed to reflect on where I was not living full but status quo and that takes courage. My courage didn' t come from me it came from my times with God and his wonderful grace and kindness towards me even in my weakest moments reminding me of who I was in Christ. I desperately needed to re-connect to God, prayer and the Word of God. **We can be involved in ministry and easily lose connection with the Lord of ministry. We prevent this by constantly doing a tune-up on our relationship with Jesus and shying away from pointless religion and works that involve God but are not about God' s agenda**. The Word of God is the revolutionary instrument with which breakthrough can occur. With that being said, let us courageously move forward by being open to act like our paramount model, the epitome of breakthrough, Jesus Christ.

Most times people expect us to have it all together and even if we don' t, we wear masks as if we do have it all together. If we are honest most of the time we do not have it all together but again, we try right? You can take it off yourself or the trials of life will help you remove it because you will get so tired mentally and emotionally of people pleasing and perfectionism you' ll just throw it out of the ring in exchange for God' s peace, direction and real grace. Once you remove the mask you are ready to begin your breakthrough journey. Needing a breakthrough feels like the 11th round in a boxing match and you are getting pummeled by your opponent and ready to pass out on the mat at the next punch. Our mouths are ready to say I quit, but for anxiety sake we suffer in silent frustration. I remember a time like this in my own life, I felt like I did not have a friend in the world and my situation was suffocating me. I was trying to be the best wife, mother, minister and every other hat I wore yet I did not feel successful at all. My contributing factors I was striving, performing and meeting everyone else' s needs accept mine. I' d lost my value and in some cases never knew my value so couldn' t truly embrace the abundant life Christ died for me to have and live. I' d come to a place where I needed to find my value, my vision and my voice! I was also tired of dumbing myself down to make others feel comfortable while I suffered in silence. This suffering silence is easy to do especially if you are involved in church going or ministry in my experience, because if your problems are too messy people shy away from you and tell you to just pray. Praying is fine but I needed somewhere I could un-robe spiritually and naturally, be myself, get wise counsel, strengthened, some honesty and truly re-aligned in my life and ministry. I was sick and tired of feeling like a caged bird. **God spoke to me one day and said no more. He said, "I want you to find your identity in Me, stop dumbing yourself down and walk in your purpose." It serves no one when we play small. With this command, the women' s ministry he gave me was conceived, Wise Women Win.** It would be a while before it was birthed but it was conceived in prayer and seeking God for my life. I wanted to share my plight but just did not feel safe enough to just yet with anyone. There is safety in a multitude of counsel yet even with this there is balance. Intimate details can only be shared with those mature enough to handle the weight and sensitivity of your situation. **When you are dealing with marriage and ministry problems you need skilled physicians not practicing physicians. If this happens to be your situation be led to trusted leaders or even therapy to solve issues talking to any and everyone is un-advised.** I cried what felt like a river until I could cry no more, and then something happened. I opened my mouth not to cry but to speak, I said, "I am more than this; I am more than a conqueror." As I rose to my feet I felt the enemy' s purposes were disappointed and the God was lovingly nodding his head in approval of his princess saying, "That' s my girl." My situation did not change right away but my mental position did and those words gave me the strength to get up, start moving and even begin looking for a new plan. Words are powerful. They are full of life or death.

Faith comes by hearing, and more importantly hearing the word of God, (Romans 10:17) so you will believe what you hear. Know this that principle works both ways, whether the words are faith-filled or fear-filled you will believe one or the other, I chose faith that day and encourage you to do the same.

Scripture says, "Life and death are in the power of the tongue (Proverbs 18:21)." Our speech gives us a glimpse of what is in our hearts and minds. If we will experience breakthroughs we must fill our minds with the Word of God and faith in that Word. **You' ll have to be like that trapeze artist in the circus; letting go of the bar in the back of you to grab what' s in front of you!** God is attracted to His word to fulfill it, so we need to believe and speak the Word of God if we will see our manifestation. Continue to speak the Word of God when emotions are raging and it looks like all is lost. It is in this place of uncertainty, when it looks like God is nowhere to be found, **speak by faith.** Speaking by faith puts pressure on your situation line up with the promises of God and it builds your personal faith. Say out loud, "God I can' t feel you but I know you are with me because your Word says you will never leave me."

As you do this you put faith pressure on your emotions to sit down and shut up. Some of us have been sold the lie that we cannot control our emotions, especially women. We can be emotionally intelligent beings that glorify God in our emotions because He gave them to us. You are also pronouncing a blessing over yourself when you declare the scripture out loud and the more you do this the more you will be assured that God is with you. You will know that God is with you, because He will confirm His presence every time, he confirms himself many times over to his servants in scripture. When we go through turbulent times, emotions tend to run high and we can easily succumb to their power to dictate our decisions. During emotional times is where we muster the strength to put emotions at bay and make some smart choices. When we have a tendency to be more emotional giving into our feelings is not wise but pushing past feelings into the realm of faith will benefit us greatly. Let' s be honest sometimes we will lose it emotionally but where sin abounds grace does much more abound. So where we have greatly messed up God can greatly clean us up and he doesn' t need our help. The devil will never beat God and you can always repent with an honest heart and start again. **Give yourself grace to continue to move forward, you can do it.** You may not be able to do that on your own, if possible pick up the phone, call a mentor, prayer partner or just someone you trust and talk through the tough time.

Begin to research in the area you need a breakthrough from the bible, reputable on-line bible studies, sermons, small groups, daily conversations and more. **Yes inundate your mind with scripture and times of quiet prayer and meditation and apply the whole armor of God to yourself daily.** By simply declaring that you put on each piece by faith, the helmet, the breastplate, the shield of faith, the Sword of the Spirit and the Gospel shoes of peace you are mindful to be aware of attacks from the enemy. Be alert for opportunities to try to move in a new direction and move forward. A good listening ear can do wonders during a tough time. People don' t always need to give you an answer but sometimes just listening to a new take on a situation can stir up the resolutions you' ve been looking for. **It also helps when talking to someone to express how you are feeling and, get it out so, you can then begin to make sound decisions.** I have learned that once God gives you an avenue to share something, it is for your healing so you don' t have to keep revisiting it but stay in forward motion by forgiving and pressing toward your goal. Even the Apostle Paul said, "I press on toward the goal to win the prize for which God has called me heavenward in Christ Jesus." The Greek word (dioko) press here is to properly, aggressively chase like a hunter pursuing a prize or pursue with haste. **The Apostle' s attitude toward past and present glories or tribulation was to keep pursuing his goal with haste and not get stuck in either extreme.** According to Jeremiah 1:12 it is God' s word that he fulfills, not our moaning, complaining, doubt or unbelief it is our response to profess his Word that brings about the manifestation of His promises. There is nothing wrong with crying and God he hears our cries, but if you are looking for results, signs will follow them that **believe**, not them that only cry. We simply have to come into agreement with God' s Word and if it is tough ask God to help your unbelief, I have many times before. Life can be hard but I am reminded of the Word in Isaiah 50, when you do not know what to do, simply trust in God and lean on him awaiting your next directions. God will give you peace, take it!

I have good news; if you are exhausted and exasperated then you must be close, close to a breakthrough. One of the hardest things for us as humans to admit is that we need help and that we are not the masters of the universe! When we don' t admit we need help or where we are truly failing we only repel what we truly desire in life and relationships. Admit it! **We are also afraid to admit to God that we are mad at him for what we feel like is taking so long to get us to our help, healing, deliverance or any other good thing that would help us at the moment. Believe me, He can handle it and he already knows what you are thinking any way. If you are feeling this**

way it is a good time to pray and tell God all about your disappointments in Him, yourself and others it will be a great relief and starting point to victory. A disappointment is a feeling that you've missed an appointment with someone or something. Allow God to give you some new desires and divine appointments. In Psalms (139) it tells us that God knows every word altogether in our mouths. This does not mean to speak to God and only complain, but pour the complaint out and then get God's Word on the thing and pray the Word over the barrier. Praying and speaking God's Word penetrates the tough areas of our lives. Meditate and speak the Word until you believe the Word. Faith comes by hearing, so speak the Word so you can hear yourself (I write this several times because it works) and finally see what you have been saying. The word breakthrough in itself implies that there is some type of barrier in our lives and a sudden advance is needed to leap into fulfillment and victory. When you come to the knowledge that you need a breakthrough, it doesn't matter in which area, but what matters is you are almost near the end of a seemingly dark valley. It is usually in the valleys of life that we tend to reflect to point of realization that things must change. Valleys can become plush and rich in vegetation but it does not mean we want to stay there forever. Mush!

Be encouraged and hope in the Lord. We have the power to look up in expectant hope and to change our minds. Any day above ground is a good day! Every day alive we can speak faith-filled words with an expectation to change ourselves and our situations. If Christ died for your salvation which is the ultimate act of love how much more do you think he wants you to have a good life? We cannot create supernatural breakthroughs but we can embrace them when God sends them into our lives. The right thoughts; God-thoughts bring about the courage to take the right actions. When we believe right things it' s only then that we will act right. Trying to act a certain way without truly believing what is being acted out will never prosper us. It sounds all too easy right? One person telling you to think happy thoughts, this is not the same thing. God' s Word is full of power.

When you change your mind to think like God and obey his instructions you will see change. Jesus teaches us to "Have faith in God" in Mark 11:22. Jesus himself encourages us to use our faith as a means to remove problems and difficulty. God is a good God and he wants you to release your faith and believe His word and accept His Word as truth, when you do this you will see results. We must also actively build on our most holy faith (Jude 1:20), how you say? Build up your Christian faith by studying and obeying God's word and also praying in the Holy Spirit. Faith in God will carry you through situations and it will deliver you from situations. Hear God, he is a real-time God with real-time solutions. There is a peace that comes with doing this.

As believers we get the opportunity to pray as led by the Spirit in accordance to Gods' will as revealed in His Word; which breaks barriers in the spirit realm. We live in the three dimensional physical world and there is a spiritual realm. The spiritual realm is just as real as the natural realm. How do we know it exists? The bible says, "Praise to God and father of our Lord Jesus Christ, who has blessed us in the heavenly realms with every spiritual blessing in Christ. For he chose us in Him before the creation of the world to be holy and blameless in his sight" (Ephesians 1:3-4). The Holy Spirit helps us to pray the perfect will of God. **Know that rote, uninvolved faith and prayers will not produce much, if anything at all. To experience breakthrough our prayers must be energized with faith and passion.** God said in Jeremiah, "Call to me and I will answer and tell you great and unsearchable things you do not know." Unleash your faith in prayer right now!

"Father in Jesus Name, I confess my unbelief. Please forgive me. I have had little faith or even worse no faith in you. Please forgive me now and cleanse me from all unrighteousness. I ask you to please stir up the measure of faith you have already given to me. Help me to use my faith to see your kingdom come. Set my faith on fire that I may serve you and experience you in new ways. Set my faith on fire that I may experience the breakthrough I need so desperately. I take my eyes off of the situation now and put them on you. I

trust that you know what is best for me. Your will be done. Amen"

Now that you' ve prayed and rededicated your faith, let the freshness of God' s promises come out of your mouth instead the ruins of negativity. God acts upon His Word, so keep it coming out of your mouth! People will make fun of you and tell you that it doesn' t take all that but the person who will experience breakthrough will go the extra mile to practice good spiritual discipline. He watches over His word to perform it (Jeremiah 1:12). God gives us all a measure of faith (Roman 12:3); it is up to us which level of faith we will activate. Our gift of faith is enough to do what we need to in order to have victory in every situation. Some people in the bible had little faith (Matthew 8:26), others faith (Mark 5:34) and even more great faith (Matthew 15:28). Jesus Christ is the ultimate forerunner of faith; he set a sinless example to show us how to finish our faith-walk triumphantly. Jesus Christ is the Author and Finisher of our faith (Hebrews 12:2).

Faith in God' s Word changes us and our situations from the inside out. When we choose to walk by active faith, taking God at His word and being obedient we walk in kingdom authority. The Word of God has living power and it is energetically efficacious, cutting with double-edged power. You will see change because His Word is alive, not dead.   Too many negative thoughts can cause you to be like an over-trained athlete becoming exhausted, exhibiting poor performance and derailed success. One good thing about being exhausted is that you are forced to stop and reflect. **A moment of truth buds from your lack of inner strength and gross self-dependence. In valley moments when you are weak, you realize, now I truly need my identity in Christ (not a religious mask), hope and active faith.** Don' t get it twisted, when you need to go to the next level, there will be *work* and determination involved. Know that God is not the type of God to leave you to work things out in your own capability, that' s love. His perfect love casts out all fear (1 John 4:18), accept his love and move forward. Ask yourself, "Have my fears ever helped me?" If the answer is no, then start using your faith for the breakthrough you need. Point your faith in the direction of the breakthrough you need. Grab hold to the promises of God and point at them with laser beam faith. Because we know He loves us we do not have to fear rejection, separation or abandonment. I've experienced them all and God is not like man, he will not leave you when life gets too messy. If you do not completely stop, reflect and receive God's love you may hit a psychological pothole and spiral downward into being depressed, critical, judgmental or even worse bitter. If you are not sure if God loves you, let's pray right now.

"Father in the name of Jesus I thank you for loving me unconditionally before I could even love myself. I confess I don't always believe that you love me or feel like it. I sometimes need your love so near, like a blanket on a cold day because of my frailties. You are faithful to your Word and you love me. I know this because your Word says that you so loved the world you sent your Son Jesus to die in my place for my sins. You also show your great love to me by allowing the Holy Spirit to place your love in my heart. I am accepted in the beloved, which is Christ Jesus. Please let the billows and waves of your love roll over my soul

right now and may I always be assured of your love for me from this day forward no matter what I am going through. Amen."

Here is where faith must kick in afresh because you will have to not only change your mind but discipline your mind to be renewed about whatever situation you are going through. If it is marriage, renew your mind about marriage, if it is finances renew your mind there. You will need to stand for something at this point and put away any self-pity. Normally only two people come to a pity party, you and the devil. Cancel that party and receive God' s grace and direction to move forward. Now is not time to default and be defunct but to decide. I am no therapist but I do know what it feels like to be tired of being tired which is a hallmark for setting your sights on new beliefs, new practices and new direction for your life. God' s promises through His Word will be revealed to you and new hope will be birthed in you as you decide. **Once you set your mind on breakthrough, own it, make it your priority!** Listen for God' s new directions and strategies;

the smallest steps in the right direction can sometimes make the biggest difference when you are going through a tough time. As you settle it in your mind that you will not waiver at the promises of God you will gain new expectancy, which is a breeding ground for momentum, manifested promises and miracles. In the scriptures the woman with the "issue of blood" believed and hoped that if she could not touch Jesus himself but just the hem of his garment she would be made whole. Her reach of faith towards him was recognized by him and rewarded with breakthrough healing power for her life! Desiring true breakthrough can lead to a road of self-discovery and God discovery, it is a great journey. As you hope in God you will sense the atmosphere around you changing both inside you and around you. Hope is contagious!

Author Portia Nelson paints a wonderful picture in her poem about self-discovery and how we can feel and react when we truly need a breakthrough in our lives. The poem reads like this:

I

I walk down the street.

There is a deep hole in the sidewalk.

I fall in.

I am lost ... I am helpless.

It isn't my fault.

It takes me forever to find a way out.

II

I walk down the same street.

There is a deep hole in the sidewalk.

I pretend I don't see it.

I fall in again.

I can't believe I am in the same place.

But it isn't my fault.

It still takes a long time to get out.

III

I walk down the same street.

There is a deep hole in the sidewalk.

I see it is there.

I still fall in ... it's a habit.

My eyes are open.

I know where I am.

It is my fault.

I get out immediately.

IV

I walk down the same street.

There is a deep hole in the sidewalk.

I walk around it.

V

I walk down another street.

Breakthrough Street

You might not have all of the answers yet but you can begin to move in a new direction. Like the author wrote in her poem, "Walk down another street", *Breakthrough Street*." **I believe a contrary circumstance is one of God' s ways of waking us up to another chance.** Problems are usually precursors to where our true potential lies. Move away from the chaotic mindsets, emotions and move toward faith in the Word of God, prayer and obedience! True supernatural breakthrough will come by prayer, obedience to God's Word and *the power of God working for you.* It is time for grander thinking. How can I write or say this? Because this book was written during a time I desperately needed breakthrough in several areas of my life, my career, marriage, finances and myself. I felt I was being defeated on every hand and feeling a holy discontent. I knew there was more. When you get close to a breakthrough the adversary will try everything and anything to wear you out so you stay distracted from the true purpose of a thing. Distraction is a big tool the enemy uses to keep our focus off of the main thing, the breakthrough. He will use family, friends, the store clerk, husbands, and wives etc. to cause you to desert your breakthrough and remain in bondage to thoughts and habits that profit you nothing. He will try to lie to you and accuse you of negative motives. When the enemy comes to speak to you or accuse you tell him to shut up and get away from you! Jesus did, he said in Matthew 4:10, "Away from me Satan! For it is written:

Worship the Lord your God, and serve him only."
Satan your enemy is determined about killing, stealing from you and destroying you. He wants to keep us deterred from the truth as long as possible so he can keep deploying his lies into our lives hoping we will believe them which is why it is so important to be armed with truth. So we must cut his suggestions off at the root and in the beginning before his lies have the opportunity to take root in our minds. Believers must let it be known that we do not acknowledge his attempts to sway us from our faith by rebuking his voice and affirming our love and loyalty to God alone.

We as believers must be even more stirred and passionate to gain our victory and breakthrough than the devil is to keep us from advancing in God' s kingdom. Before Jesus went on to work his earthly ministry he was tempted of the devil but he broke through his lies by using the Word of God. Although Jesus' time of testing may have caused some weakness due to hunger or tiredness he still spoke God' s Word. He gave us a great example; even when you are tired speak the Word only! You might not have to scream at the devil but after life' s situations have slapped you around enough you will begin to get bold in your faith and your soul will cry out, "No more!" This cry for "no more lies" will invoke a spiritual warfare and at this time it will be a necessity to continually fill your mind and your mouth with God's word so the Lord can fulfill his promises to you.

We will ebb and flow on by the priority that we place on God's Word in our lives. So it is essential to do like it says in Hebrews 10:23, "Let us hold fast the profession of our faith without wavering, for he is faithful that promised." When we do this we are essentially saying to God, "I am in agreement with you on this promise for my life. We have come to the same conclusion about my victory and I have the courage to proclaim it out loud so I know I will see manifestation of the promise!"

The enemies of your success will even try to make you feel comfortable in an environment you know is not thriving like toxic bacteria in poisonous pond water. As we know toxins are poisonous to humans. Toxins to the believer are lies of the enemy that penetrate our thoughts and begin building stronghold's so the truth cannot enter. Toxicity can also come in forms of all types of relationships. Toxic relationships tend to deplete you and be abusive to you emotionally or physically.

Toxic relationships need to be identified and extinguished to prevent hindering your new advances. Sometimes that is easier said than done and I won't say a lot on the subject but what I do know from people who have been in toxic relationships is this; they decided enough is enough. Studying and hearing the Word of God is like introducing spiritual antibodies into our minds, situations and problematic behaviors. The Word proves this because Paul the Apostle states, "So then faith comes by hearing and hearing by the Word of God." The spiritual antibodies, if you will, identify and neutralize the foreign deception of the devil making room for the truth which sets us free.

The devil uses things like; lack of discipline and diligence keep us from our breakthrough. **Breakthroughs require perseverance, period.** We will consistently have to fight the good fight of faith because a true breakthrough is trusting in

God's power over your own ability. **If we will have a breakthrough a renovation of the soul is a requirement as well. Soul prosperity will help you enjoy the new strides you are making.** We prosper as our *soul* prospers, that is what we call soul-prosperity.

Our soul, in short, is our mind, will and emotions. In order to be totally free to experience breakthrough a decision to being committed to confrontation is needed. Confronting any emotions that back-fire on us and cause us to lose ground will help our agenda for revolutionizing our situations. **Breakthrough discourages negative habits that steal our time and energy.** So in essence we not only have to be sick of the difficulty but sick and tired of our own negative responses that cause our troubles to weigh in the balance instead of being successfully stabilized. Be honest, if we are remaining in a dead situation, we are by default evading a breakthrough by wallowing. The area in which we experience tumultuous times, no advancement, retreat, no growth and as a matter of fact it feels like you are in quicksand, is an opportunity to break out! **Failure means a lot of things but one thing for sure that it means is; you can try again.** The wall is coming down because when life gives you a choice you will either wallow effortlessly or you will realize I am too tired to even wallow, I must make a decision to find or do something new. Joshua said this, "And if it seem evil unto you to serve the Lord, choose you this day whom ye will serve; whether the gods which your fathers served that were on the other side of the flood, or the gods of the Amorites, in whose land ye dwell: but as for me and my house we will serve the Lord." Make a decision to believe, "You are of God, little children and have overcome them because greater is he that is in you, than he that is in the world (1John 4:4).

Truth always demands a response. It is time to give your life an overwhelming response with renewed hope and faith, breakthrough is waiting. You will come to the conclusion it' s do or die for me and the verdict is in; I choose purpose, I choose me and I am taking my power back. When a person comes to the point of choosing God' s purpose and choosing themselves over drama they are already on the brink of a breakthrough. It is on the brink of breakthrough that you realize I do not want this mountain of unproductive negativity I am ready to live in my true value, vision and voice. Through the Word of God we have the tools to change and win!

Realize resistance is real

The bible tells us to submit to God and resist the devil. Who is the devil anyway? A created angelic being designed to bring glory to God but he got the idea that he would declare war on God and ended up getting kicked out of heaven (Luke 10:18, Ezekiel 28:1-19). He fell from the presence of God and he wants believers to fall from that place as well. Why do we need to resist the devil? We need to resist him because he strongly resists our victory. There is an unseen war going on whether we will acknowledge it or not so being neutral is not an option.

The devil takes a complete stand against you in the faith to see you defeated. But glory to God we are fighting from a place of victory because Christ took our place on Calvary we can appropriate his victory in every one of life' s battle' s. To prove that Colossians 2:13-15 Message Version reads like this, "When you were stuck in your old sin-dead life, you were incapable of responding to God. God brought you alive— right along with Christ! Think of it! All sins forgiven, the slate wiped clean, that old arrest warrant canceled and nailed to Christ' s cross. He stripped all the spiritual tyrants in the universe of their sham authority at the Cross and marched them naked through the streets." How' s that for a day of success?

Jesus was speaking to Peter and he informed him that he was being sifted as wheat. Here is how the conversation went, "Simon, Simon, behold Satan demanded to have you that he might sift you like wheat. But I have prayed for you, Simon that your faith may not fail. And when you have turned back, strengthen your brothers (Luke 22:31-32). In the verse, the attack was to put

Peter through spiritual sieve and remove his most spiritual useful assets. Jesus' solution was to pray for him! You then must realize you are being attacked! But why you say? Have you asked yourself, "What have I done to anyone or what am I doing wrong?" Most likely nothing but it is a reality of a believer. So be assured an enemy is coming against you that is resisting you reigning in certain areas of your life! Please do not spend all your time focusing on darkness and the devil. Focus on Jesus Christ and simply be aware. Once your anointing is evident the devil will do everything he can to block new areas of success breaking through in your life. The devil wants to keep a breach open in your life that allows him access to you but God wants to possess the breach and annihilate the enemy on your behalf. Think about it, any great kingdom ever worth having was attacked by an enemy who tried to steal the ownership rights of the empire. For example, Jesus Christ represented the kingdom of God fully in every way. As a baby Jesus was granted divine protection. Herod the Great had a diabolical plot to kill him because he was a threat to his place of power. God has enemies and we do too! Psalm 2 says this, "The kings of the earth rise up and the rulers band together against the Lord and against his anointed saying, 'Let us break their chains and throw off their shackles." "The one enthroned in heaven laughs, the Lord scoffs at them." No matter the time period any exercise by God's enemies to overthrow him is an exercise in futility but it has never stopped the enemy from trying to abort God's purposes.

In the book of Matthew, Herod the Great, a, king, was troubled because another king was sought after besides him, by wise men, that king was Jesus Christ. Herod was threatened by the prophetic words written about Jesus and did not want to see his government come into rule. In today's language, Herod started to freak out because his light was dimming and the Great Light, Jesus Christ was coming onto the scene. Believe you me, Herod did not have a John the Baptist sentiment which says, "Let me decrease so you might increase". We too have a place of power in Christ and the devil knows it; which is why he will try to do everything in his power to keep you from moving forward and taking dominion in your life.

Our place of power comes direct and only from our position in Christ Jesus. Look at the how the scripture describes the power in us, "Now unto him that is able to do immeasurable more than we ask or imagine, according to His power that is at work within us." Wow, there is power at work in us as believers and God is able to do the unimaginable through us for His glory! This power that the scripture speaks of is the Holy Spirit that is constantly at work in a believer' s life seeking to produce great fruit in us as we are yielded to him.

As soon as we begin to set up the kingdom of God in our own lives and heart we will be attacked by the powers of darkness. When King David in the bible was anointed King the Philistine' s got mad, scripture states, "And when the Philistines heard that David had been anointed king over all Israel they went up in full force to search for him, but David heard about it and went out to meet them." When David' s enemies simply heard he was appointed (set apart for office) and anointed (consecrated for office) they got upset and deployed attack.

There was no way they were going to let David' s government be set up easily. When our enemies see our decision to serve the Lord and come into unity with His plan for our lives, enemies will gather forces and attack. One more scripture here, remember when Joseph, the dreamer, told of his dreams to his brothers in Genesis 37, the bible says, his brothers hated him all the more! When Joseph told his dream he was put in a pit, taken out of a pit and even worse sold to traders. Right here we learn the principle that sometimes when we expose our dreams prematurely to those around us they get upset and retaliate by trying to make us conform to life' s hollow experiences selling us a counterfeit dream for our lives.

Please note the enemy will use wiles and strategies against us to build strongholds against our mind' s ability to gain new insights that will cause us to produce new realizations and accomplishments in our lives. Believers are an automatic threat to the kingdom of darkness because the more we act, talk, walk and do what

Jesus Christ commanded us to the more territory we take from the kingdom of darkness. Most times we do not even realize how much the devil is threatened by us, which is why he will try his best to keep us depleted about our true identity in Christ Jesus. Jesus proves this principal when he spoke to Peter in Matthew 5, he said, "Now I say to you that you are Peter (which means rock) and upon this rock I will build my church and all the powers of Hell will not conquer it." Jesus was not just reminding Peter of his name because Peter forgot it; he was pronouncing and imparting Christ like identity to the apostle.

Our true identity in Christ is more powerful than the enemy on our worst day as believers. Sometimes the reason we stay defeated as believers is we lack discipline. God has done all he is going to do on our behalf spiritually, now it is left up to us to appropriate the great grace and abundance we have inherited through our connection with Jesus Christ. Jesus said in Luke 10:19, "I have given you authority to trample on snakes and scorpions and to overcome all the power of the enemy, nothing will harm you." That is an amazing promise and it is ours as Christians to exercise on a daily basis against all that opposes us when we are walking out our purpose in God. We must consistently ask ourselves, "What level of life do I truly want to live?"

Changing our minds and thinking differently is imperative so that we will do differently when it concerns our lives. We must change our mindset to agree with God' s word in order to see answered prayer. Now get in the Word and study on the area you need a breakthrough in! The Word of God is alive and powerful very much able to cut away the mind sets that inhibit us from moving forward in our God given call and life as a whole. A breakthrough will take some work on our part too. The Word of God is able to convert us, convince us and then comfort us on our journey. We literally need to be a people that take God at his Word. Think about it, the bible is speaking to two sets of people, those who believe and those who don' t.

God is constantly urging us by His Spirit to believe what His Words says so we can have what His Words says! The Word of God is alive to help us experience the God-kind of life he designed for us to have through Christ. Romans 8 declares that all God' s children are heirs and joint heirs with Jesus Christ, so all the Father has is ours both now and in the future. The price Jesus Christ paid for our ability to have breakthrough is priceless so it behooves us as joint heirs with him to be diligent about living an overcoming lifestyle. The book of Hebrews says it like this, "The word of God is alive and active, sharper than any double-edged sword it penetrates to dividing soul and spirit, joints and marrow, it judges the thoughts and attitudes of the heart."

The Word of God can be used defensively like penicillin to heal us from generational or present spiritual bacteria that keep us from being our best self. So putting our minds and hearts under the microscope of the Word of God regularly will rid us of behaviors that will not benefit our believing lifestyle.

Realize this, spiritual attack will commonly look like bad habits, procrastination, and resistance to victory from family or friends

or our own reluctance to move forward. This is a plumb line showing us where we need to make adjustments. You will have to come to terms with yourself in order to see true breakthrough. Does that mean that God can' t or won' t move until you take self-inventory? No. God does want you to maintain the integrity of your breakthrough by dealing with matters that frequently deter your soul- prosperity. Commonly you might hear someone say, "I just feel stuck!" Speaking words like that let you know that you need God' s help.

Feeling stuck is normal; don' t let the enemy wear you out with the thought that you are the only one or you should be farther along. Regret leads to depression; ask me how I know that? I know because I spent months beating myself up because my life didn' t look a certain way and all I was doing was wasting more time grieving over things I could not change. Regret is a trick don' t fall for it because has no treat at the end. Regret only leads to depression. The antidotes to this type of attack is to simply get moving, (a body in motion stays in motion) if your thoughts can stagnate you, your momentum for life will be lost. I have learned one very important thing and it is this, "Master me first" . Forget about what everyone else is doing and learn to keep your word to yourself. Don' t simply have faith for your future; put your faith to work for the now too! If you fall, just get up and try again. Its ok to make a mistake just don' t keep making the same mistake; after the first time it is no longer a mistake it is a choice. It is most profitable to stop competing with others because your journey is unique to you! We will always have areas of weakness but the key is to know those areas and strengthen them. If you only play life to your strengths you will become unbalanced and more than that develop a false sense of identity and worse become prideful. Some of the most successful people fail first before they take off in the realization of their achievements. Failing in itself is not bad but not learning from the experience and repeating the same mistakes over and over again now that' s bad. Avail yourself to the notion that the very problems you are having are a precursor to your coming into your promise. The trouble could be exactly what you need to make feel sick enough to say enough is enough, I am going to do something about this. Fall forward.

Losing momentum will cause us to "idle", like a car. Idling in itself is not bad nevertheless research shows that a car that idles excessively can actually damage your engine components. To add to that, research has also proven this bottom line: A car that is in an idle position more than ten seconds uses more fuel than restarting the car. So, what am I saying? I am saying it will cost us more to keep our lives in an idle position than simply starting over again. Even if you simply move in the direction of reading your bible, getting wise counsel or prayer at least you are moving. Do not damage your life by being work-shy about your breakthrough! The Word of God says this in Ecclesiastes, "When the clouds are full of water it rains. When the wind blows down a tree, it lies where it falls. Don' t sit there watching the wind. Do your own life-work. Don' t stare at the clouds. Get on with your life." A mindset that says "I am expecting my pie to fall out the sky so my life can magically change" is faulty thinking. At some point you will have to put God first and trust that as you take steps of faith he will meet you with the help you need. Effort is required and not the effort of busyness but the effort of intentional effectiveness. A breakthrough in any area of life will require movement and it is shy of wisdom to think we will have no part in our breakthrough. Life will bring us all to a place where our situation supersedes our intellect and it is at this point we must trust God for the outcome that works best for our good. It is at this place of trust that God can employ His supernatural power on your behalf.

God knows your enemy is bigger and sometimes wiser than you so you are not expected to go the battlefield without His Word and His weapons of warfare which are mighty *only* when used through Him. Know this, as we seek to infiltrate our minds with God' s Word, renewing the spirit of our minds and speaking God' s Word to our impassable state of affairs, destruction will turn to Satan' s kingdom! The scripture teaches us that David prayed when he was under attack and asked of God, "Will you give me the victory?" God answered David and told him, "Yes, attack and I will give you the victory." The kingdom of the enemy was plundered by prayer!

Ask, Seek, Knock

Persistence pays off. Jesus said this in Luke 11:9, "So I say to ask and it will be given to you; seek and you will find; knock and it will be opened to you." I love the persistent widow in the bible who kept knocking on an unjust judge's door to get justice from her enemy. The judge finally gave in because the woman troubled him to point he gave in to her request (Luke 18:1-8). Jesus said we should pay attention to what the judge said, "Hear what the unjust judge said. And shall God not avenge His own elect who cry out day and night to Him though He bears long with them. I tell you that he will avenge them speedily."

Prayer is the language of faith and it is God's desire to answer us according to His will. God's will is his best choice for us when we choose our will it may not be the best choice for our lives. Scripture promises when we pray according to his "will" he hears us. Our faith will be tried yet praying in faith to God helps us to remove self-imposed limitations and move into the supernatural help of God. There are different kinds of prayer but the one that I am speaking of is the intimate time with God where you bear all in faith, simplicity, and praying in line with God' s word.

The prayer of faith brings about a peace in our hearts and establishes us in God. A defining trust will canvas our lives when we exchange our life need for God' s promises. God answers prayer. David' s sentiment from Psalm 138 says this, "In the day when I cried out you answered me and made me bold with strength in my soul." So God not only answers prayer but He strengthens you in your mind, will and emotions through relationship with Him.

Prayer is paramount both before and after a breakthrough. The very reason you need a breakthrough is because you are experiencing resistance. If you have been too tired or frustrated to pray, simply start again, talk to God. Prayer is not only talking to God, it also talking with God in which He will refresh, restore and direct you in any given situation. As believer' s the Word promises us that our steps are ordered by the Lord. Prayer is talking to God so when we talk with God as with anyone else, we also posture ourselves to listen so we can hear others' thoughts and heart concerning a situation. As the Spirit of God gives you an impression or picture in your spirit follow the influence of the Spirit. When we walk in divine direction by faith we see results, we see God's plans for us unfolding before our eyes. God does and will answer prayer, look at this wonderful promise (1 John 5), "This is the confidence we have in approaching God: that if we ask anything according to his will, he hears us. And if we know that he hears us—whatever we ask—we know that we have what we asked of him. It takes patience to walk with God because he may not do what you think he ought to do about a matter but he loves you more than enough to address the matters of your heart.

God will also give you a strategy for every issue and sometimes part of that strategy involves actively waiting not on God but with God. If you are praying His will you are simply waiting with Him in prayer, praise, obedience and worship to see your answers manifested. When you wait with him you don't get mad because he is taking too long, you wait with him in relationship assured He has the best choice in store for you. As you wait with God you gain confidence in God and get to know Him intimately. Part of a successful prayer life is simply getting to know more about the God you are walking it out with in this lifetime and the next; cultivating a strong relationship. Waiting may be your strategy for the time being. Sometimes we need to ask like David in (2 Samuel 5), "Shall I go up?" Meaning, "God I need to know exactly what I need to do in this battle right now." And if it is to wait, surely God's word says to stand still, trust God and see the salvation of God.

You begin to trust Him more than yourself because He is God. Realizing God is greater than you and His plan for your life is far superior to your plans. This is a definite walk of faith. Even though he will give you instruction you will still have to apply your faith in any matter you believe God. Did not the priest who were about to cross Jordan have the instruction to put their foot on the banks of the river, yes they did and yet they still had to exercise faith to do it. They could have said, "Well we do have these instructions but is God really going to take us over on dry land", the miracle on happened when they trusted and obeyed.

Prayer precedes a move of the Spirit, which is needed for a breakthrough. Look at this scripture, in Acts 1:14 constant prayers of believer' s preceded the outpouring of the Holy Spirit in Acts 2. The prayer experience will always work for your good. Look at John 14:13-14, it records: "Very truly I tell you, whoever believes in me will do the works I have been doing, and they will do even greater things than these, because I am going to the Father. And I will do whatever you ask in my name, so that the Father may be glorified in the Son. You may ask me for anything in my name, and I will do it." There are so many facets to prayer and one of them is the means for obtaining what we need. We do not ask so that we can consume it upon our lusts but we ask because we have a sincere need, we seek for what is missing, we knock on the door for that which we feel shut out and we seek for that which we feel shut out. Remember that as you stand asking to forgive anyone an offense so that unforgiveness does not stand in the way of your answers. Scripture explains you cannot try to put new wine into old wineskins. We must not think we can have miraculous answers or even simple help if we harbor unforgiveness, sin or bitterness towards another. Jesus wants you free, for the simple fact that freedom in God is available. He does not want you free so he can make you pay some astronomical price and divert you to works that make you strive for his blessing. We need to accept the grace of His freedom for the simple fact that he paid the price at Calvary to free you from sin' s grip. Jesus wants you to remain free because it belongs to you.

Ask big, ask bold, because answered prayer is God' s will. Praying the Word of God is speaking God' s language. Over the years I have prayed God' s word over my children and family and seen results. Danger hit my family October 31, 1998 and could have potentially stolen the life of my husband and my son Christopher. A drunk driver hit them at 70 miles per hour. I was laying on the couch Halloween night and all of sudden the phone rang about 11:30 pm. On the other end of the phone was my husband hysterically ranting and raving about not knowing if my son was going to wake up. My heart sank and it felt like the room stood still as I breathed in and out slower and slower. All I can remember him saying was, "We were in an accident, Chris is on the ground and he's not getting up and I feel like I am going to pass out, my head, my head!" I started screaming, "Where are you? Where is Chris?" A woman by the name of Marie got on the phone and told me where they were. She explained that the ambulance was arriving and that my husband was sitting by the car and my son was lying in the grass near I-5."

I called my parents because the accident was near their home. They called me when they got there and two of the men in my life were being placed in the ambulance headed to Harborview Hospital where I met them. I didn't know what to expect when I got there. My son was unconscious and my husband lay on the table with glass in his face and blood everywhere. I was in need of my

God for a miracle because I was shaken to my core. I met with some people and after that Jerry and Chris underwent a lot of testing. While that was going on I began to call on Jehovah-Raphha my Healer and Jehovah-Shalom my peace. When tragedy strikes your prayer life gets real personal; you want God to know the sound of your voice and you definitely want to hear his. I decided in those crucial moments, I was standing in symphony with the Word of God. For three days I didn' t go home and my new three month old daughter was with me most of the time. For three days I went from the 3rd to the 9th floor at Harborview talking to Jerry (my husband) and Chris (my son), caring for them and praying over them. I was determined that my family was coming home so I stood on the Word and I prayed. I remember being in the elevator exhausted so I leaned against the door and whispered a prayer, "God get me through this, help me." God gave me strength. My son remained in a coma for four more days. The doctors called specialist in from the university to consult his case because there was no reason he should still be in a coma. When they left I prayed again and I knew God was with me, his presence and peace were evident. I felt the presence of angels and I knew I had help from Heaven. The Holy Spirit was helping me intercede and Jesus was interceding for us throughout this time. God' s mercy was so rich; I knew He' d spared their lives for purpose. I was going to go home and rest but "the mother" in me couldn' t do it so I stayed, there were no beds available in the ICU so I slept on the floor and put Heaven in the chair in her car seat. I didn' t waver. He woke up on the seventh day in the hospital, praise God! Those doctors came back and when they did, my son was playing video games! I just praised God and stared at him as he asked me for some candy.

I literally laughed out loud, God answers prayer and he takes care of his own. We all went home with some bumps and bruises after nine days in the hospital. When I crossed the threshold of our home, I sighed a sigh of relief because I knew I had gotten in touch with the Great Physician himself and he diagnosed and treated this situation with a miracle for my family! To God be the Glory for the things he has done and if he did before he can do it again.

Prayer releases God' s power into our needs. The results of prayer come through a provision, open doors, closed doors, wisdom, protection and so much more. Praying to God can also give you a hunger to see more of God and more of his powerful hand at work in your life as displayed in the Word (Jesus Christ). The more you pray and talk to God the more the Spirit has access to sanctify you and make you more like Jesus Christ.

You can also repent in prayer. I know that' s a word we don' t hear a lot about any more but it is still relevant to our walk with Jesus Christ. Repenting is a change of mind so you don' t keep repeating the same behaviour that separates you from God and/or other relationships. Repenting and turning from sin brings you closer to God and gives you the ability to see the will of God clearly. Repenting also brings times of refreshing in your life. Sometimes our prayers go unanswered because we have unconfessed sin in our lives, look at this in James 4,

"When you ask you do not receive because you ask with wrong motives, that you may spend what you get on your pleasures." If all we are going to do is ask God for stuff and money to spend on our lusts then we need to repent and return to the true motive of prayer which is to see God' s will be done with a humble heart. Prayer from a longing heart that is full of faith, unrelenting and razor sharp will see God' s response to the matter at hand.

Deliberate and Decisive

Hope comes in cycles but the key is to get on the hope train every time it pulls out of the station. Sometimes we simply need to be reminded that it is an option to hope again. Hope allows you to see what you believe for and most times we remove the fact that faith is the substance of things *hoped* for and then the evidence of things not seen. Sometimes our hope will wane in hard situations but scripture simply instructs us to "Hope in God", just do it; hope. **Be deliberate and decide to hope in the promises of God.** Hopelessness breeds despair and despair breeds the arrogance that you are the only light or revelation in a given situation.

The more clearly you see yourself doing something new or being new the more you will see yourself leaving a useless situation. You have the ability to bounce back because the Word says, "I can do all things through Christ who strengthens me", and with his help you can do it! You can deliberately invest in yourself and get better. Most times we are holding ourselves back from breakthrough and saying no to who God truly created us to be in this lifetime. We let the past, lack of priority, and people get in the way which can prove to prevent us from executing our life assignments. The reason we do this is because we still fear the true expression and grandeur that God created us to take shape of, even David said,

"I am fearfully and wonderfully made and my soul knows it (Psalm 139:14). **I once heard a preacher say, "If you let go of good you can lay hold of greatness."**

A man of God once told me the problem with the church is we live too much from event to event and not enough in process. What does that mean? It means every time you have a bad day or event you get stuck in the event instead of living in process and maintaining your faith and confidence in God to know if he did it before he can do it again. Just because we experience bad events that does not mean that is who we are and that is all our value equates to. In life we will have problems both small and great even some that bring us to our knees. We must realize God had a plan before we had problems.

Crying out to God is ok, even the Word declares crying scours our heart (Ecclesiastes 7).

Crying cleanses the soul. Our tears are like the release on a relief valve letting out excess pressure to give us some emotional relief. I' ve gone through seasons of crying and weeping because words could not verbalize the breaking of my heart. Our tears are important to God. He stores our treasured tears in His bottle (Psalm 56:8). The seriousness that crying brings on helps one to come to grips with what is important. For example, I was going through a relational transition with someone I thought viewed me in a respectable light. Until one day they spoke some extremely harsh words to me and after the meeting I cried because I felt like David when he said, "Even my close friend who I trusted who shared my bread has turned against me" I was angry, almost devastated but after I stopped crying I made some decisions.

So that is what I mean when I say **a sobering cry can help you see a new reality.** I made some changes that day and set some boundaries for the types of people I would call friend. Maya Angelou says, "When people show you who they are, believe them! Pain and crying in a tough time clear the sedation we' ve been experiencing and help us to see the unblemished realities of any given situation. If we are crying we are most times facing ugly realities and that' s a good place to be if we want a breakthrough. We can go on after a good cry. So after all is said and done we will simply have to make a decision to refuse to play the starring role of the victim, get it out and move on. I am not downplaying pain I am saying at some point we will have to be deliberate about our healing. We have to be like the caring mom who knows their child has had too much candy and tell them "no" so they won' t get sick. Too much leniency can cause rebellion so giving you too much time crying can cause self-pity or depression. **There is a time to weep, a time to laugh, a time to mourn and a time to dance therefore we must be tuned in to what time our appointment with crying is over.** After a season of crying comes joy! So by deciding to get up we proactively lay hold to our next victories. When we are all done crying we must position ourselves to dry our eyes and hear God.

So with that, go ahead and literally cry out to God but is very important to hear what God wants you to do in the timing he wants you to do it in. The right move and the right time are like a perfectly fit hand in glove. Remember the story of the four lepers in 2 Kings 7, although they were very sick they portrayed a positive attitude and after some deliberate decision making ended up bringing a blessing back to an entire kingdom. The story says this: *It happened that four lepers were sitting just outside the city gate. They said to one another, "What are we doing sitting here at death' s door? If we enter the famine-struck city we' ll die; if we stay here we' ll die. So let' s take our chances in the camp of Aram and throw ourselves on their mercy. If they receive us we' ll live, if they kill us we' ll die. We' ve got nothing to lose." So after the sun went down they got up and went to the camp of Aram. When they got to the edge of the camp, surprise! Not a man in the camp! The Master had made the army of Aram hear the sound of horses and a mighty army on the march. They told one another, "The king of Israel hired the kings of the Hittites and the kings of Egypt to attack us!" Panicked, they ran for their lives through the darkness, abandoning tents, horses, donkeys—the whole camp just as it was—running for dear life. These four lepers entered the camp and went into a tent. First they ate and drank. Then they grabbed silver, gold, and clothing, and went off and hid it. They came back, entered another tent, and looted it, again hiding their plunder. Finally they said to one another,*

"We shouldn' t be doing this! This is a day of good news and we' re making it into a private party! If we wait around until morning we' ll get caught and punished. Come on! Let' s go tell the news to the king' s palace!"

What do you have to lose by trying something new, learning a new discipline, I will tell what, nothing? **One way to get unstuck is to move in the direction of your passion.** What do you like to do, what are you passionate about? One day, I asked an elderly woman in our church what she liked to do? She said, "I don' t know I never took the time to get to know what I like to do." I was astonished that she had gone through life and been so many things to so many people but never deliberately took the time to get to know herself or even what she liked to do. After that night in women' s ministry she decided to find out more about herself and what she liked to do. You don' t have to figure it all out in one day, ask God daily, "Which goals do you want me to move toward today?" Do something different, take care of you! His grace is sufficient for each place in your life.

Like the story said, The Master had made the army of Aram hear the sound of horses; they panicked and left their camp, leaving the reward to four lepers who were in no position to receive anything because they were unclean. So how much more are you a blood bought believer of Jesus Christ in a position to receive a blessing and live under the blessing of God at all times. In this case a positive attitude and a decision to move motivated four unclean lepers to success. I always say my glass is never half full, no matter what it looks like, it' s full! I believe like David, "He anoints my head with oil and my cup runs over (Psalm 23). A great attitude and good decisions can pay out great dividends, just like a sour attitude can subtract our opportunities. Be deliberately positive, because you have help in the Lord.

We must realize in needing a breakthrough we are not out here aimlessly wandering, though we are being resisted in some way, we have help. We have one that has gone before us and broken through. Jesus was deliberate in his decision to sacrifice his life for us, there was no grey area. Let me explain, Jesus Christ has made a way for us to come before God in peace and in that way being made he has provided us with priceless promises and inheritance within the kingdom of God. Therefore, since we have been justified through faith, we have peace with God through our Lord Jesus Christ, through whom we have gained access by faith into this grace in which we now stand. The scripture is sharing with us that we are justified because of Christ and all God' s blessings flow to us through Christ Jesus. I like to say it like this, "Just as if I' d never did it." Because the Jesus Christ, "The Breaker" has gone before us to justify us before God we now have peace with God.

Through Christ' s work on Calvary all hostility between us and God has ceased, so how much more will he bless us with what we need? We are no longer enemies of God but friends by grace. This is a great gift and any promise added to this great gift of salvation is pure benefit on our part. To take the richness of God' s love toward us even further, Romans 8:32 questions us, "He who did not spare his own Son, but gave him up for us all--how will he not also, along with him, graciously give us all things?"

God' s love toward us is so premeditated and on purpose that to think of it too long is phenomenally mind blowing. It is not God' s idea to give us his best and then make us squander the rest of the way, He will provide. He is a God who sticks by you and walks with you through good times and bad, He is faithful! Again He already gave His best in Christ so what is it to Him to provide a need, or be a comfort or answer a prayer? He didn' t hold back His best so why would He hold back the rest? If God has given us his greatest gift will He not give us the lesser of meeting our earthly needs or spiritual request? Everything we need has already been provided we simply need to lay hold of it through prayer with thanksgiving.

A little more about Jesus Christ "The Breaker" , he will go before you and behind you to protect you in every spiritual battle. The minor prophet Micah gives us a little insight on what I and others call the breaker anointing. Micah' s name means, "Who is like Jehovah?" speaking to the fact that there is no one like the one and only true God who alone defeats our enemies completely. *No one can help us gain the victories we need except for God.* Micah declares in his prophecy to the oppressed, a time of restoration after judgment of their sin. Micah spoke to God' s people a time of restoration after chastisement. **Just because God corrects does not mean he does not love you on the contrary, he corrects because He loves you.** In Micah, deliverance is promised to God' s people by **a breaker.**

The breaker, who is the Lord Jesus would overwhelm and destroy anything that stood in the way of His people's restoration. It is amazing to know that once God has decided to break through for you nothing and no one can stop Him. Scripture tells us that God is the same yesterday, today and forever (Hebrews 13:8) so what he did then, he will still do today for his covenant children today.

The Greek relevance for this word breaker (parats) is to break through, make a breach, burst out, grow, increase, press, open or scatter. **The people's release from captivity came because the breaker went before them to overcome every one of their obstacles preventing them from freedom.** Look at how Micah recites the promise to Israel, "The One who breaks open the way will go up before them; they will break through the gate and go out. Their King will pass through before them, the LORD at their head." Once the Lord Jesus Christ goes before them the people will then break through the gate and go out! Christ has already trailblazed us out of exile through salvation so how much more *every* spiritual battle we must fight until we see him again.

We should meditate upon the word of God that says, "In the Messiah, in Christ, God leads us from place to place in one perpetual victory parade. Through us, he brings knowledge of Christ (2 Corinthians 2 Message)." How amazing that God can use jars of simple clay to bring forth the exquisite and powerful message of our Savior! Faith shifts us from the anxiety of setbacks to believing and then seeing the enemy's advances crumble before us because of God's power at work for the believer. God doesn't simply give us the victory, but His defeat of the enemy is like a procession of victory by a great king through the city. **It is through the life of a yielded believer that the progression of the kingdom advances and the wonderful knowledge of Christ are expressed to others as a sweet aroma.** God wants us to have victory! Our victory comes because Jesus Christ has already made the way and now we need to appropriate the blessing to see deliverance. The Master Breaker breaks a way for the captives through their enemies and breaks down anything that hinders His people from restoration to God's perfect will. He is still doing it for us today; declare now, "**God is breaking through for me!**"

We learn in Micah, that God's people who have been in captivity cooperate with the breaker to come out of bondage and so must we cooperate with the strategy of God today to break out of restricted situations. The master of breakthroughs awaits our call, it is His will to give us an expected end that glorifies Him and fulfills the plan of God for our lives. The Message version (Micah 2:13) of scripture conveys the idea like this, "Then I God will burst all confinements (restrictions; to keep within limits) and lead them out into the open. They'll follow their King. I will be out in front leading them." God breaks out against our enemy to lead us out of bondages and things that restrict us and hold us back from His perfect will for our lives. Praise God!

God is in the business of deliverance and we know this because he sent his only begotten Son, Jesus Christ to redeem us back from the state of sin bringing us back to peace with Him. **He broke**

through the sin problem with the ultimate sacrifice to get us our freedom once and for all. Deliverance is not just deliverance from demonic advantage but also delivering you to a prophetic place of purpose in a new dimension. God can get you where you are supposed to be no matter how much time you feel you have lost. Someone who experiences true breakthrough will follow God' s lead because they know they can trust Him. Once we understand that God is for us we are headed for victory! The breakthrough comes when the power of God goes before you and behind you, this means his constant presence is with you!

God gets behind you to hide you from the enemy, making it impossible for him to advance. God goes before us to be our light, making us ready for which ever direction he chooses to lead us. The Word declares God' s Word is a lamp unto my feet and a light unto my path (Psalm 119:105); the Lord will precede you and take fixed position behind you to gain you the victory in your life. He loves us! God desires our freedom because he tells us that Christ liberated us to be free, so we should stay free (Galatians 5:1). So although in life we encounter problems we need to understand that our heavenly Father' s mind toward us is always to be free from the enemy' s attacks and restrictions. Jesus Christ paid it all for us to be free and privileges us to have life and have it more abundantly. Life abundantly means God' s plan for us is to have life (physical and spiritual) and to live an all-around blessed life which exceeds ours and others expectations. He is the God of excess!

God doesn' t just want to deliver you and bring you out in a meager way; he wants to bring you out with a high hand. Scripture teaches us that Israel came out with a high hand (Exodus 14:18)! What does that mean? A high hand means that God wants you to come out of trouble and transition highly exalted above your enemy with your hands open in praise to God based on the fact we trust Him. If God brings you half the way, he will take you the rest of the way, he wants to bring you out of adverse circumstances with his power, direction and means. He wants you to come out boldly and confidently trusting in his might and knowing he defeated the enemy before the trial began. This type of triumph reminds me of Jesus display of success against Satan. The ultimate conquest is described like this in Colossians 2 (Message), "He stripped all the spiritual tyrants in the universe of their sham authority at the Cross and marched them naked through the streets." Also in Ephesians 4, Jesus Christ' s definitive defeat of Satan is described like this, "He climbed the high mountain, he captured the enemy and seized the booty, and he handed it all out in gifts to the people." Wow, talk about a public display of victory over the devil. Jesus also gives believers authority over the enemy, Luke 10:19 (Message), "See what I' ve given you? Safe passage as you walk on snakes and scorpions and protection from every assault of the enemy. No one can put a hand on you." We are protected and have power over all the power of the enemy through Christ, praise God!

God is described as the possessor of the breach (2 Samuel 5). To possess something is to own it and control it. What an amazing thought that God owns the exact thing that is causing you trouble. He owns it and is waiting on you to take possession of it, for the kingdom of God. I'm reminded of how encouraging Caleb (one of the twelve spies) was in his positive perspective when it was time to possess the land of Canaan. He said, in retort, "Be quiet everybody, the land is amazing and full of milk and honey and don't get me started on how incredible the fruit is over there." He continued by saying, (my paraphrase), "Hey, it's huge and well put together and we even saw what looked like giants and all other types of people but come on, we are well able to take it because God is with us." Joshua and Caleb (Numbers 13 and 14) went to Canaan with 10 other spies, who in essence said, "We can't do it, we can't take these guys they are much stronger than we are, take our bad report and stay here. Furthermore, the giants there will devour us, I mean you should have seen them, they were huge and we were like grasshoppers. Forget this mission abort it now people, stay with Team Grasshopper and you will be safe." What a gigantic chasm between belief systems! Two people on the team said, "We got this, we can't lose with God on our side! The other ten said, "Abort the mission we already lost." To truly see breakthrough giants must become insignificant and the Word of God the ultimate authority. This also teaches us today that as believers in order to get the job done for God, we will not always need the majority just a few on fire believing saints.

Even though it looks like the enemy is in control in a certain area of your life and he may be (due to our disobedience, perspective or ignorance) but God is ultimately in control. Knowing that you are ultimately fighting a defeated enemy because of Christ Jesus' s victory at Calvary can help you gain proper perspective and insight to win! Give yourself a break you don' t need to win the world overnight. Again, by Jesus' death, burial, resurrection and ascension he completely conquered evil powers and has given you authority to stand as His earthly ambassador. God owns the breach that enemy keeps using to come through or into your life; you just need to receive the fact that Jesus cancelled the contract between you and the devil. Armed with this knowledge you dispossess the enemies of

God off of whatever territory you need to regain. How do we do that? Firstly through prayer as we discussed previously because when we get in trouble our first response should be to go to God because He holds the strategy to defeat every enemy.

Preparation for that Place

Wouldn' t you like anything more than to see negative schemes the devil plots against you annihilated and see the enemy of your soul crushed under your feet? Me too! God did this very thing time and again for His people in the Word of God. He has given us the power to break negative cycles in our life by prayer, the blood of Jesus, faith in Him and His Word. **It will also take our desire to choose acknowledge our cycles and get off of the rollercoaster of repeat.** A lot of times this means leaving cozy comfort zones that really only work against our progress. Leaving comfort zones means acting in faith to do little by little what we are dreaming about! Our faith is designed to work together to completely bring to life the transformation of your situation. James so eloquently, says it like this, "For as the body without the spirit is dead so faith without works is dead also." Our faith is like our body and our works are like spirit just like a body without a spirit is lifeless so our faith without some works is lifeless and of little value. We must be persuaded by the

God-kind of faith more than we are our belief in our ability to fix things. God's persuasion (faith) plus your confidence (faith) in Him works together to produce what He prefers for our life, His best choice for our lives which is His perfect will for you. Sometimes it's hard for us to believe the best because of hindering mentalities.

Our blessing can be staring us in the face and we miss it because we are not living in the present tense but we are still stuck in the presence of the problem when God has released the solution. To be prepared for breakthrough you've got to be willing and teachable. Look at this example about Peter the Apostle who was placed in jail because King Herod was persecuting the church. Herod arrested Peter, put him in prison and handed him over to be guarded by four squadrons of soldiers intending to mock him further in front of the people. The story goes like this:

Then Peter came to himself and said, "Now I know without a doubt that the Lord has sent his angel and rescued me from Herod's clutches and from everything the Jewish people were hoping would happen." When this had dawned on him, he went to the house of Mary the mother of John, also called Mark, **_where many people had gathered and were praying_**.

Peter knocked at the outer entrance, and a servant named Rhoda came to answer the door. When she recognized Peter' s voice, she was so overjoyed she ran back without opening it and exclaimed, "Peter is at the door! "You' re out of your mind," they told her. When she kept insisting that it was so, they said, "It must be his angel. "But Peter kept on knocking, and when they opened the door and saw him, they were astonished. Peter motioned with his hand for them to be quiet and described how the Lord had brought him out of prison. "Tell James and the other brothers and sisters about this," he said, and then he left for another place (Acts 12).

When the servant girl, Rhoda tried to explain that the people' s prayers were literally answered in the person of Peter standing at the front door they didn' t believe in the power of their own prayers. By their prayer and intercession the church broke through the heavenly realms and impacted the earth realm with angelic assistance. Apostle Peter was delivered supernaturally then gave the church instructions to testify of God' s goodness and left for his next assignment. I believe this incident left an imprint on the church at Mary' s house to look for answered prayer instead of doubting it no matter who delivers the good report. Are we ready for God to move in this type of supernatural capacity in our lives? Are we prepared by believing, are we ready? As a young woman, I lost my driver' s license to tickets and for a long time I did nothing about it but drive illegally. Don' t do that! After giving my heart to Jesus, the Spirit would gently convict about getting certain areas of my life in order, this was one of them. I had no idea where to start then one day I overheard a gentleman talking about his license and how he got them back. I thought I wonder if that will work for me. God had me at the right place at the right time. I was supposed to hear that conversation. Faith rose up in me to get my license back only one thing; I didn' t have the money to pay the tickets. I moved forward in faith by writing a letter to the courts explaining my situation, apologizing and asking for mercy because I wanted to drive legally. I was getting prepared for that place! I got a letter in the mail from the court system stating they would not re-instate my license. I sat on the front porch and prayed God, I can' t do this without you, show me how, I don' t have the money but I desire to drive legally. God, I am hoping against hope. "Well, days later I got pulled over by police. I explained my situation and told him I was truly working on getting this matter together. He told me to wait he was getting a call after calling my plates. He came back to the car and said, "I' m going to let you go, your driver' s license has been re-instated! I was prepared and the Breaker went before me and gave me unmerited favor. I went to the DMV with the biggest smile and praise for God in my heart. I was legal again. The breaker anointing was setting my life back in order even back then. I prepared myself for a breakthrough by confronting a tough situation and believing God for the best outcome.

While going through situations, you will also be changing from the inside out, transforming to be more and more like Christ. God' s grace also being involved is more than enough to help us with what we feel like are special cases, like Peter' s. In other words don' t just **go through it, grow through it** by submitting to the Word and power of the Spirit. **Meditating on the word and soaking in the word will prepare us for triumph.** It will give us a sense of expectation. God' s grace is His unmerited favor and kindness towards us as his people. Grace is free; we can' t earn it, which makes it ever advancing, free, ready, quick, willing, and prompt to all men who will receive from God. Our status can change, as our mind changes so our situations will change. **God is a strategist and He wants you to win in life!** I believe this because the Word calls me "more than a conqueror" which signifies success. The scripture says it like this in Romans 8, (31-32, 36, 37) "What then shall we say to all this? If God is for us, who can be against us? Who can be our foe, if God is on our side? He who did not withhold or spare even His own Son but gave Him up for us all will He not also with Him freely and graciously give us all other things? Even as it is written, for thy sake we are put to death all the day long we are regarded and counted as sheep for the slaughter. Yet, amid all these things we are MORE than conqueror' s and gain a surpassing victory through Him who loved us."

Our victory is already complete and set upon the precipice of fervent prayer, believing and working our faith in obedience to a God whose methods may change but he Himself does not change (Malachi 3:6). Although we go through many things, we are assured by God' s comforting words that we are perfectly loved and never alone thereby making our victory a lifestyle and not simply the occasional occurrence. Psalm 54 teaches us that we will be delivered out of all our troubles and will look in triumph on our enemy. Get in agreement with God.

Jesus Christ comes to go before us in any and every battle, even as he did for Joshua entering the Promised Land. Check this out, "Now when Joshua was near Jericho he looked up and saw a man standing in from of him with a sword drawn in his hand. Joshua went up to him and asked, "Are you for us or enemies?" "Neither," he replied, "But as commander of the army of the Lord I have now come." Then Joshua fell facedown to the ground in reverence and asked him, "What message does my Lord have for his servant?" The commander of the Lord' s army replied, "Take off your sandals for the place where you are standing is holy. And Joshua did so. You are probably saying, "What does that have to do with breakthrough?" Well I will tell you. Each time we as believers get ready to embark onto new territory we will have two encounters; one with the enemy and one with God.

As Joshua stood with his gaze to ground as do many of us when we have things on our mind, he looked up and saw a man with sword drawn. God is always willing to be to us what our faith requires so we are strengthened for the journey. Joshua went over to him and began to ask the man, "Whose side are you on?" because Joshua was courageously in "fight mode" . The man gave no military strategy only His rank and assignment. Jesus commanded the scene by letting him know I am not here in any capacity that you have mentioned I have come to you to be over you as Commander, not partner. Jesus was letting him know I am captain of the Lord' s Army to go before you and I do not fight in this Earth realm, you do. You have been fighting and I am letting you know I am with you. Jesus in this specific case came to remind God's man that He was with him as a leader and would be giving him strategy as he went into Jericho to conquer the land not to grapple with military assignments of the day. Jesus said to Joshua in essence, "I am not coming to help you or harm you; I am coming to take the reins as Senior Chief of God' s army and go before you to give you the victory on all sides.

God came and made himself known to Joshua to assure him he was not alone. The first part of gaining the victory is being convinced; our God is with us and that He is holy and His reign is supreme. In response to the Lord, Joshua the general worshipped the Commander of the Lords hosts, next in all humility he dove in to ask direction of the Commander. In other words, "**I am in need of a breakthrough; you are in control, what you want me to do.**" Joshua showed his inward expression of worship outwardly by removing his shoes, which to me signifies that he respected the encounter he was having with God and he also relinquished his stance to guide his own steps. God made a promise to Joshua in earlier chapters (Joshua 1:5) to be with him and here God is being faithful to fulfill His Word. By his presence God was preparing Joshua for breakthrough after breakthrough in the Promised Land and so it was time to cross the threshold by divine strategy and possess the land.

Are you ready to allow God to take total control in order to experience the breakthrough you need? If you are, it' s time to connect with God and observe the God that is truly on your side. Like the Prophet Joel shouts, "Proclaim this among the nations: Prepare for war! Wake up your elite forces. Let all the soldiers draw near. Call them up." Accept your position of being redeemed and act like it.

When you have a complete yes for God the enemy will do everything in his power to prevent you from becoming unified with the purpose of God and becoming established in God to fulfill your kingdom mandate. The devil and his antics will try to keep you smothered with distractions so as not to see God or clearly see your assignment. Again, 2ND Samuel 5:17, "But when the Philistines "heard" that David had been anointed king over Israel, they went up in full force to search for him, but David heard about it and went down to the stronghold." History says David went down to the stronghold to rally his troops.

Sure enough if you are need of a breakthrough you will need time to retreat and strategize spiritually and naturally to accomplish the orders of God that bring you breakthrough. If you are appointed and anointed to fulfill God's purpose and you are, the devil has heard about you! When the devil hears about you being anointed (painted and perfumed with the Holy Spirit to go about doing good) he is going to try to spread himself out all in your life to get you distracted with putting out fires everywhere so that you will never achieve God's will for your life or help anyone else. You may even get stuck in relationships that are full of religion and other time waster' s to keep you from your God-given assignment. The enemy' s goal is to debilitate you with circumstances, fear of the unknown, lack of knowledge and over run emotions. When attacks are fierce you can feel like you will never accomplish God' s goals for your life. Remember this, the devil is a created being too and he can only do what he is permitted. You can pass any test thrown your way being armed with the knowledge of the Word of God. So start speaking a language God understands, it goes like this, "Lord you said in your Word so and so and I thank you that the request is fulfilled because, I believe I receive it, it is so. Amen." Take authority.

There are those days you feel exasperated and wonder how I am going to follow through with God' s strategy when everything looks and is so intimidating. You ask yourself, "How in the world am I going to get to the other side of this when the situation is so daunting. Simply believe. God will send help! David must have cried, "I need help" when the Philistines "***spread***" themselves out in the valley of Rephaim (2 Samuel

5:18). The Hebrew connotation for the word spread (natash) here is to smite by implication as if beating out and expanding and also to abandon. These definitions make perfect sense to me because I am sure as large a company as the Philistines were they seemed even bigger to David as if they started out as a large ball but then pounded out to expand right before his eyes. And we have all been in situations where we feel as though we are against the ropes being pummeled by our opponent and abandoned by God' s supernatural power with no help in sight. The sight of the Philistines or maybe even a message got back to David and probably left David feeling abandoned which pushed him into prayer for a line of attack against this great army. Inherently, emotions are not bad yet when it comes to decision making we need not let them lead us into any unwise choice that could potentially delay our destiny. What if David would have simply fled the scene without consulting God? Running away could have simply prolonged the situation and ruined his reputation as a leader. So it behooves us to not only stop and think but to pray as well. Feelings can cause you to slip back into the stagnancy God pulled you out of in order to position you for purpose. So make sure you check your feeling-o-meter before you decide to leave the brink of a breakthrough you have worked so hard to attain. Listen of course to THE SPIRT but also to your spirit. A wise woman once asked me during a tough time in my life, "What is your spirit saying?" Essentially she was saying follow your place of peace, real peace and not what you want it to be. Let the peace of God rule. Let it be the umpire that calls, safe, out or foul ball in your emotions and decision making.

The part of you that is connected to God spiritually is your spirit and that is how He communicates with you. The Spirit itself bears witness with our spirit that we are the children of God, that' s Romans 8:16. The spirit of a man is the candle of the Lord, searching all the inward parts of the belly (Proverbs 20:27). So instead of yielding to your emotions or frustrations yield to the Holy Spirit and also let the peace of God rule or umpire in your heart. Do you have a knot in your stomach, then that usually means NOT to move forward with that decision, do you have His leading and His peace then He probably wants you to move forward. We get caught too much on what it looks like and what people think that honestly are too many voices speaking! Get still and hear what God is saying to your spirit. That problem you're concerned about, He is saying, I got you, you can be sure that I will take care of everything you need and my generosity will exceed yours, be still, I am coming. Yet you hear all your emotions and your mind racing which you are so used to that you let them lead.

This is where you have to take a bold stand and retrain your spirit to lead and your emotions to follow. Emotions on edge will wake you up in the morning talking about, " So, what are you going to do about that?" These accusations will lead you right into fear but again here is where you need to retrain your emotions to take a back seat to your spirit man. Follow the truth, follow your faith and take a bold stance for lifestyle of faith and the blessings you know only come from you trusting God! It's tough, I know but you know what, its do or die right now because when you pass this test you can become an advocate for someone else to help them along the way if they get weak in their faith. You can share with them how God is faithful to His Word and he watches over it to perform it. Close the door to allowing your emotions to lead, follow your peace and stand up for what you truly believe God's Word is saying to you! You are on the precipice of a total life change if you are reading this so just accept it and follow God's peace. It's cliché but He really didn't bring you this far to leave you now, He's not that kind of God. He is intentional about getting you to the right place at the right time. You need to just go ahead and declare, "I am going somewhere in God" that way you set the atmosphere for everything in you and around you to line up with God's perfect plan for your life. Don't retreat! Why he took you or me this route for breakthrough I am not sure but I do know Joseph made it perfectly fine from the pit, the prison and onto the palace perfectly pruned just fine and right on time.

David got a word from God about being attacked by the Philistines and that is all we need to move forward, one word from God! Put your expectation in God. In Matthew 8:8 the centurion spoke to Jesus in this manner, "Lord I am not worthy to have you come under my roof, but just say the word and my servant will be healed." The Greek word logo as defined by Strong's means a word, speech, divine utterance or analogy. The Roman soldier believed Jesus Christ's words had enough power to procure a miracle for his servant. The soldier believed that Jesus simply speaking would emit godly power into the situation and deliver healing to the person! He obviously had great faith in Christ and in his power to perform miracles. **The Roman soldier attributed omnipotence to Jesus and believed that if he spoke the simplest of words it would prophetically travel through space and time to accomplish a supernatural deed in the body of his servant. No wonder Jesus said, he had great faith!**

True breakthrough requires getting rid of a grasshopper mentality and taking on giant-like mentality. What we meditate on and say shapes our reality daily. **If you see yourself as winner you will be, if you see yourself as a loser you will be.** Allowing fear and natural perspective to dominate you will bring death to intended blessings God has stored up for you. The enemy will always try to trick us by making us believe we have lost something when he already knows we already possess it. His attacks will be focused on your belief in God and belief in His Word. As we think in our hearts so we will be in our lifetime.

Some of the spies in Numbers 13 came back with a bad report, they said, "We seemed like grasshoppers to ourselves and to them." Wow, they were already defeated before they even gave themselves a chance to crossover to the new land because they had grasshopper mentality. They saw themselves as small and just decided that, that's how other people saw them as well. The enemy wants to keep your focus on the problem or other formulas so that your faith in God is reduced to uncertain hopes. Religious formulas only cause doubt and confusion. In other words don't have faith in faith have faith in Jesus! With faith in Jesus you can see beyond the facts and you will get to the other side of your dilemma, hallelujah! The scripture (2 Samuel 5:20) says, "And David came to Baal-Perazim (possessor of breaches) and David defeated them there. And he said, "The Lord has broken through my enemies before me like a bursting flood." I go back to an original question asked earlier, "How will I get to the other side of this?" The Lord is going to go before you and put a breach in the ranks of the enemy's army so you will discern exactly where and how to attack and you will say like David, "The Lord has burst through my enemies". Remember God promises in Micah 2 to assemble his people from captivity and gather them as a remnant. He promised that he would put them together like sheep in a fold and everyone would hear them because they multiplied in captivity. God said, he would open the breach and go before them so they could *"breakthrough"*. This reminds me of Psalm 23, "The Lord is my shepherd, I shall not want. He makes me to lie down in green pastures. *He leads me*, beside still waters. He restores my soul. He leads me in the path of righteousness for His namesake. **Each**

stanza starts with He, letting us know that God will lead out when it comes to blessing because He is a blessing God. He leads us into places of prosperity i.e., green pastures, still waters, restoration and righteousness. This is what God wants us to believe so that we are transformed by grace in a close relationship with Him not just some behavior modification that only frustrates our plight to win. This type of prosperity is His perfect will for our lives, God is a good God, hallelujah!

God has to be enough. The Kingdom of God is already in us so we should be applying those principles' to see God's favor. Always use God's principles mixed with faith then God has a legal right to get involved in your trial. Breakthrough requires trusting God completely with the matter. Breakthrough requires hearing God on the matter and being disciplined enough to follow through on what you've heard, speak it and then see it manifest. Keeping our thoughts on spiritual realities will help us to see physical manifestations. Sometimes life and situations can utterly exhaust you but God is faithful to send help. That help may come through a word of encouragement, a song or even much needed rest. The victory God has given us over our enemies should encourage us in the faith. If you truly have Christ you may feel down but you won' t stay down because the Greater One lives on the inside of you. Blessed quietness will come into play as you advance into breakthrough, trusting God' s word and ability to deliver. It is tempting to try and fix things on your own but that will only make a mess. One of the enemy' s tactics is for you to keep responding to his plans and plots of foolishness and intimidation. Only move forward in your God given strategy by faith not fear. God did not give us a spirit of fear but of love, power and of a sound mind (2 Timothy 1:7) and we must make the decision to believe, confess and receive God' s word on the matter. The more the fires of affliction you endure the more sober you will become.

Attacks come for the Word' s sake. What do I mean? Psalms 105 says it like this, "Until the time came to fulfill his dreams, the Lord tested

Joseph's character." Let's remember the story in the bible, Joseph had a dream and he told it to his brothers and they got so mad about it that they put him in a pit, then sold him off to traders, and then lied about him being killed. There were other factors going on in this family but we'll talk about that dysfunction in the next book! Off Joseph went to Egypt to be tested for his dream-sake but more importantly to serve his purpose by going before his family to preserve life in the land through his gift of government and administration. His delay of dream was simply his training for reigning. Word planted in our heart will produce faith. The word in our lives serves to make us more like Jesus so as we reign in our purpose we are not just looking the part but acting like Jesus while doing the part. God wants the Word to work in our lives. God wants our heart and mind in agreement with spiritual reality concerning our situation. I know it can be hard; the situation is completely contrary to what God's word says! This is where you use faith-muscle; keep speaking the word, living the word and believing the word just like pumping iron. This is the time the word of Lord is testing you in whatever dream God has given you, it is testing your gifting and character. And just like Joseph when the time is right your gift will make room for you; you will be released and promoted! Faith will never deny physical reality but being in harmony with the Word impact the physical realm. In times of testing God is simply testing His Word in you so that when you come out your faith and your words are purified. A holy indignation will hit your spirit and it will proclaim, "Enough is enough!" I will no longer continue to play the devils game because I keep losing, no, I choose God and I will win. How can you say that? Scripture says, "It is God, who always causes us to triumph."

The victory is already ours we just have to come to that determination. David waited until God moved; but not until then. He was trained up in dependence on God from his providence while taking care of his father' s sheep. God performed his promise, and David failed not to improve his advantages. When the kingdom of the Messiah was to be set up, the apostles, who were on assignment to beat down the devil's kingdom, did not attempt anything until they received the promise of the Spirit; who came with a sound from heaven, as of a rushing, mighty wind, Acts 2:2. They prayed and they waited.

Take the open door, when it is time for you to advance move! Standing in the shadow of your pain or dilemma will only distract you from true purpose. I knew God wanted me to write books and he kept tugging on my spirit to get busy. For so long my catch 22' s and pain kept me paralyzed from producing. Move in your spiritual reality by thanking God for the answers. You don' t need to see the whole idea just begin taking steps toward your vision. Bottom line I was procrastinating. I needed to confront that unhealthy behavior by bringing to Jesus and asking for his help.

Breakthrough requires giving your pain to God and casting all of your cares on Him because **_He cares for you_**. We all go through different levels of pain and I am not suggesting that the pain of situations goes away over night, but I am saying the more you turn it over to God in prayer the less relevant the pain will be and the more important your deliverance and freedom will become. Begin thanking him for answers and healing.

Back to Joseph for a moment, he named his son Manasseh, which means, making to forget and his other son Ephraim meaning fruitful. Joseph said, "God has made me forget all my toil and all my father' s house; For God has caused me to be fruitful in the land of my affliction (Genesis 41:51-52). **God' s goodness was so good it edited Joseph' s memory of his horrible past, and made him fruitful in his present wow!** So we do not live in denial of the past but we can neglect the past so we can pursue our future. In Isaiah 43 God says, "Forget the former things, don' t dwell on the past. See, I am doing a new thing!" God is saying do not let the past prohibit you from seeing what I am doing right now. Forget it whether it' s good, bad or ugly because the new thing I am going to do for you is going to far outweigh what I did in the past and whatever happened to you in the past if you' ll just give it to me. I just believe as God is the same, yesterday, today and forever more he is still in the business of allowing His glory and our joy far outweigh the trials we endure. That' s a good God!

Your pain will become a catalyst for your purpose. As I sat and wrote this book, I was in one of the most painful times of my life and it continued even after this book, but the power of God pushed me forward to finish this assignment despite of the pain. I know that He went before me protecting me so that I could complete what I started and be free from stagnation. I say to you, don' t quit, our pain will sometimes parallel our progress. Use your God-given assignments to study, pray and act on what He is telling you to do; healing comes this way. I felt so inadequate in so many areas but I began to roll that on Jesus and thank Him for his adequacy. I was also reminded that he uses tired people, scared people, people without resources but most of all yielded people. Ask God for strength and wisdom; he is faithful to give it to you!

As God releases His strategy and timing to you, act upon it using the prophetic Word from the Lord for the next moves in your life. Take the grace-enablement for the assignment. When God offers you an open door walk through the threshold of that door, do not waste time pondering your distractions, they will always be there. You say, "Well what about the mess in the middle? The things that I feel are happening to me that I have no control over, the people who I feel are draining me or my financial situation etc.," To that I say look to God's sufficiency and do not be caught off guard, in this world there will be troubles but your determination for breakthrough must become greater that the trouble you are facing. Move in the direction of the strategy God has given you and other trustworthy sources. When God told David to move it was essential that he did so in time or he would have missed the opportunity to pummel the Philistines and restore the ark of the covenant to the City of David.

Our loving Father in heaven gives us strategies to regain losses we have sustained and even to experience new things and seasons. While writing this book I was on a fast because I wanted to consecrate myself before the Lord for personal changes in my life, it was part of the strategy to begin to see and experience personal breakthrough. At the time I also believed for great change in myself, marriage and career. I stood on God' s Word that says, "Draw near to God and He will draw near to you (James 4:8). God can step in the middle of your mess at any moment.

I truly wanted to get rid of anything in me that was being ruled by my senses, carnality or otherwise. I wanted to know the where the root of my problems were so that I could get free and stay free. God desires to give His people breakthrough from the inside out (spirit, soul and body) so that it is lasting and not fleeting. Breakthrough also comes when we truly reflect about where we are and where we want to be so that when we receive the breakthrough we are in an honest place, able to retain the breakthrough blessings. Follow His leading into new territory even if it feels new or strange because trailing God' s direction in obedience and sometimes sacrifice will always produce safety and blessing for you. I am reminded of a songwriter that wrote, "The safest place to be is in the will of God."

Part of my personal breakthrough came when God gave me Psalms 126 to read and study. He encouraged me that there is a time and season for everything under the sun and captivity does not last always. I felt like a captive in everything, job, ministry, marriage and other things because they seemed to not be producing but God was using the frustration to point me toward revelation and breakthrough. In captivity, you normally don' t produce; you take what is given to you; in the scripture the Lords people are released from captivity by a decree from King Cyrus that the Jewish people could return to their land and communities. I am sure the captives just like me wondered, "If they would ever see their home land again and if this trial would ever end."

During this time I really began to seek God for strategy to see change and God began to give me strategies to change me first, once that started happening I viewed both people and situations differently. It was like all of sudden an upheaval started and everything was turned upside down, it was God creating situations that made me hungry to see the Word of God manifested personally, professionally and otherwise. Breakthrough is an exciting time but can be a lonely time because everyone will not want to celebrate your new found freedom especially if a person or situation has been a stumbling block to your life. Things that seemed to be so overwhelming and immense began to pale in comparison to the new found freedom I was finding in the inner healing and deliverance that was taking place in my life. It is not to say that during this time, I did not feel pain or hurt, because I did but I knew with God on my side and the assurance of his love and protection nothing could hold me back from a total breakthrough.

Just like in the Word, David defeated the Philistines by the strategy and power of God going before him but then the Philistines came back again and spread themselves in the valley of Rephaim. At this point, in my seeking a breakthrough began to feel like, "Will this trial ever end, will this pain ever go away, will I ever see the dream God spoke about my life and family?" I felt like I was in constant battle. Which made it hard for me to enjoy life but I had to begin to make changes that were not only eternal but that benefited my here and now and qualified for legacy. I needed to enjoy me and enjoy life again even in the midst of my strategy seeking and hoping for manifestation of Gods power in certain situations. Life can be a scary when you have done all you know to do and you are standing in truth, sometimes alone, but choosing faith over fear gains us ground every time.

The second time around, when David encountered the attack of the Philistines he inquired of the Lord but got a different strategy than the first. The Lord told David don' t do the same thing you did in the first battle, this time go behind them and ambush them. So it was a time for David and his men not to be seen and they needed to listen for a specific sound in the trees. After hearing the sound then they were to move out against the enemy. The sound was a signal that God was going to go before them, to smash and annihilate the Philistine camp. David did exactly what God told him to do and since he carried out this new strategy God said, "I the Lord will go **before you**."

When the power of God goes before you in your stead nothing, nothing can stop you from living in your purpose and receiving a complete breakthrough in your life. David experienced attack, prayer, a Word from the Lord, an opportunity to be obedient, a strategy, a confrontation and a victory. You will have your part to do with your breakthrough as well.

As in Psalms 126, the captives were set free and experienced a dream-like mood, unable to fathom actually going home this time of release felt like they were dreaming. They finally experienced the time of their release, their breakthrough if you will after 70 years. They were laughing and singing and gathering what little they had and heading home. I am sure this breakthrough witnessed to those around them in a great way, as will our breakthroughs in life. When God breaks through for you in a situation you absolutely know that you are the object of His love because it is to Him you have prayed, worshipped and on Him you have waited to give you ultimate victory! Nobody else can take the glory and you cannot give the glory to yourself or anyone else because when you experience breakthrough it is because you have been dealing with an impossible situation. You have been dealing with enemies that tout obscenities, dole out nothing but doubt and are crass in their confidence against you. They publicize your supposed defeat, laugh at you, and publicly humiliate you because they are most secure that your day will never come. Nevertheless the more evil audacity and impertinence the enemy displays is only a launching pad for the God of the Angel Armies to display his mighty power in your heart and life! Going through this tough time God kept sending people to remind me that though others had spoken and done some horrible things to me God was watching and He was my vindication. I still had a responsibility to foster freedom in my life and do my best to get better not bitter.

A breakthrough requires a lot of honesty and the determination and action to discipline yourself in hearing and walking out the truth in God's grace. Lies come from all types of sources and our best bet is to identify the lies that have plagued our lives so we can have the opportunity to experience real and lasting change. Where are you going through a tough time right now? Maybe that is a good place to start investigating patterns that have negative results in your life. Not dealing with issues and expecting them to go away is like living in a world of make-believe! When you do discover faulty systems in your life put them up against the light of the Word of God and draw a plumb line, that plumb line will represent a resolve to never cross into the land of make believe ever again and living in truth in all areas of your life. Put the work in to live in truth, (no matter how painful) discipline and challenge yourself to be free and stay that way. Just like drugs and alcohol will never numb people enough to make their realities and problems go away so lies will never set any one free! Any type of addiction whether lies, drugs, sex is a cycle you must choose to be free from or die. Pain is the battle to breakthrough, you feel like,

"How can I make it through the pain of being attacked like this and feeling like everything, every promise is delayed or even worse denied. While you are on the brink of a breakthrough your pain may parallel your progress but choose to keep moving forward because it is no good to try to manage pain with more pain. We do not ask the doctor for more pain when we go into his office to see him, we ask for help to get better, we ask for solutions.

Acknowledge the pain, yes I said absorb it, be honest with yourself about how bad it hurts and then cast your cares on God. Pain has the potential to go on for years and cause a person to want to be numb so it does not have to be dealt with successfully. As with everything, when there is a negative there is a positive, keep going to God and let him enlarge you through prayer and praise as you release the pain to Him. Get to the root of what is causing the pain (issues) so you can move on in life otherwise you will only be able to simply manage the pain instead of get rid of it. A lot of times we like our symptoms so we keep going back to noxious (things harmful to health) stimuli (something that incites to action) because we are in a cycle of pain. Sometimes our cycles imply that we are medicating our pain instead of seeing it cured. For example, you keep going back to that old boyfriend or girlfriend, who clearly does not make you number one in their life and hurts you on a regular basis. Even with the barrage of red flags that disrespect you, you keep taking their calls and rescuing superficial emergencies. Start unpacking your pain and get free. Yes, yes, yes start happening to life and stop letting life happen to you. You are not a victim but a victor in Christ Jesus. Let God use your prayer and praise to strangle the life out of that which seems to be strangling you! Know this, as believers we never lose, we either win or we learn. *Father I pray for anyone reading this book that you would give them courage to unpack their pain before you and other safe places so you can heal their soul and cause them to be free from stimulus to the pain and the pain itself. You came to heal, healing is our portion and by your stripes we are healed. We receive our portion now in Jesus Name, amen!*

Breakthrough requires giving your pain to God, repenting of pain you've caused and casting all your care upon Him because you can believe He cares the most about you. The pain of unpacking is sometimes more excruciating than the event itself, it's a process but it's worth the work. I can say this because the same cycle of pain kept reoccurng in my life until I decided to ask, "Why does this keep happening to me?" I turned the search light on myself and now I am experiencing freedom in areas of my life like I never knew. I found my wasy back to a healthy me and I am still finding freesom daily. In Psalms 17 (Message) David gives us a great example of how to do this he says in the Message version, "I call to you God because I'm sure of an answer. So-answer, bend your ear, listen sharp! Paint grace-graffiti on the fences; take in your frightened children who are running from the neighborhood bullies straight to you. Keep your eye on me; hide me under your cool wing feathers from the wicked who are out to get me, from mortal enemies closing in." God will never leave you and only has good plans for you. After casting your care on God, care for yourself. Make yourself a priority, encourage yourself. Find yourself worshipping God and praising Him just because He is God and watch that pain and heaviness begin to lift. I call to God on a regular basis, down on my knees crying my eyes out and confessing the pain I cannot describe but know that it is so real.

I know in my heart only an encounter with the Holy Spirit can touch our heart and lift that pain- healing our heart so that we can go on strong and healed. The pain reveals a pressure point in life that helps us acknowledge just where we are and what we need to do to move forward. Pain helps us to know something is wrong and needs attention. Pain can be both physical and emotional. Without the pain we might not ever realize we had a problem. Pain hurts because we have had something that has been damaged and needs to be restored. There are several ways to deal with pain; medication or pain management systems to name a couple. As believers we know that God still heals today because He is the same yesterday, today and forever. The Word of God declares, "The chastisement for our peace was upon Him and by His stripes we are healed." I call it the grand exchange giving God your burdens and in return you feel lighter, wiser and ready to move forward. It's like being in His presence and believing in faith thrusts you to a new place of wholeness. Sometimes that place is immediate and sometimes it is progressive; keep going. Jesus restores our soul (Psalm 23) when we are exhausted and weary. Draw near to God and He will draw near to you (James 4:8).

Again concerning Psalms 126, the freed captives were rejoicing but also begin to set a plea before God. They prayed that the Lord would "turn again" their captivity. In other words I know I'm free from this situation yet I need to be established vis-à-vis where I am going. It was very smart of the Israelites to pray about their situation because there is nothing like having freedom but no resources to support the new place you are entering. The Israelites enlisted the divine support of the compassionate and all -powerful God. What did this prayer mean, weren't they already free? Yes, but they needed the fortunes they once had in order to live successfully in the freedom recently received so they prayed! They were asking God to bless what they had so they could move forward even if that meant crying while sowing. The once bound captives were committed to wait because they were convinced that sowing and waiting would bring in a harvest for their lives. They were praying for their deliverance to be perfected to corroborate the freedom they were experiencing. Joy was clearly a part of their inheritance, since they had sown in tears they would reap in joy.

Jesus desires that our joy be full so let us pray:

Father in Jesus Name, thank you that you have given us the garment of praise for the spirit of any heaviness, we receive that garment to praise you now! We know that we are free, for freedom Christ has set us free and we will stand firm in that liberty. Thank you Lord that where the Spirit of the Lord is there is liberty and the Spirit lives with us and is in us eternally. As heirs of the kingdom of God we receive the full joy you desire for us to have. Thank you in advance for joy in the Lord that bubbles from the inside out. We praise you now for joy and confess, "I have joy now!"

Our freedom is a matter of truth in Christ Jesus. We must receive that truth as royal heirs of the kingdom of God. Soak our minds in the fact that Christ came to set us free and expose us to His victory and our destiny as kingdom citizens and royal heirs. We war and live from a place of victory and we are more than conquerors in Christ Jesus. In Genesis 38 as Tamar was giving birth one son pulled his hand back (creating a breach) and his brother Perez came out. Tamar exclaimed, "What a breach you have made for yourself!" Perez means breach, bursting forth or breakthrough. In Ruth 4:11 the name Perez is synonymous with blessing, the Hebrew word pehrets implies a place of victory. Perez is in the genealogy of Jesus Christ. Jesus Christ in us causes victory because He is the Breaker. Praise God for the breaker!

As the Lord goes before us to break out on our enemies and exterminate them we can break out in praise because we understand God knows the end from the beginning and God is faithful to deliver His children. God may not deliver the way you believe he should or in your timing but He will deliver you the way He sees best for your life as the Creator of Life. No one and nothing can be successful against us with God on our side. The book of Romans says that, "We are more than conquerors" , so what exactly does that mean? It means our deliverance is assured in Christ Jesus. It means that any trial or test that comes my way is designed for me to win and pass the test in Christ Jesus. Most times we feel like we are going to have a breakdown before we see a breakthrough but I believe in order to see a true breakthrough we must get to this point so we can stop depending on our finite solutions. This place of breakdown as I like to call it, feels like, God has forgotten about you, it feels like life is unfair, people who do bad get all the breaks, it feels like the same things keep happening over and over again with no relief in sight. You want to throw your hands up and say forget this faith stuff it is not working or God I love you but I am just going to coast right now. Everything you are feeling at this point go to God in prayer and tell Him all about it because you can completely throw yourself on him, he can handle it and he won' t let you down.

This time of repeated prayer will bring you to a place of letting it all go and coming into a peaceful trust and reliance on God. That trust stems from walking with God and learning that no lesser power can defeat his purposes for you. Let His promise to you that you are more than a conqueror inspire you to worship without holding back since God did not hold back on giving you

His heart' s best treasure; Jesus Christ. Jesus Christ is His most lavish gift given to us and if he has already given that there would be no reason he would withhold any lesser gift according to His will. As we believe right our lives will yield right results! So according to Romans 8 we are more than conquerors, we are super-conquerors! Through Christ we can prevail mightily being overwhelmingly victorious because Christ has already gone before us and gotten us the victory by His death, burial, resurrection and ascension. Jesus Christ is our pre-eminent conqueror and by His success he has launched us forward into triumph. With this knowledge we must take ownership of being part of God' s family and reap the benefits of being an heir and joint heir with Jesus Christ, our elder brother.

Desperation, Humility, Obedience

Breakthrough has been defined as a sudden increase in knowledge or understanding so I submit as we gain the truths from Gods Word and his Spirit we will experience the turnaround in our situations that we need. Extended focus in the area we need breakthrough will renew our minds preparing us for the move of God. Fasting added to prayer and the study of Gods words will also put you in a dynamic position for breakthrough in your life. Fasting and prayer can put you in a great position for breakthrough to bring about a release of God' s presence and power.

The biblical fasting I mention is a spiritual exercise where you go from the absence of food for a time coupled with prayer to experience God' s revelation and power in a specific matter. Fasting and prayer calls us to turn our attention to God and the things of the Spirit while bringing our

flesh under subjection. Fasting and prayer should surely be an option if one is in need of breakthrough. Jesus fasted and prayed (Matthew 4) to prepare for His earthly mission. There are different
versions of fasting so make your best personal informed choice and remember it is about quality not quantity, it' s the intent of your heart that matters.

Tough times will cause us to stand and look at our barriers or overcome them by understanding that God is the God of breakthroughs. **The first step to breaking down barriers is being desperate enough to get to Jesus with no pre-conceived notions that you can fix anything.** In the valley at Rephaim (2 Samuel 5:20) the Philistines raided the valley and that must have caused much confusion. It never feels good when our environment is full of confusion. The Word says, "God is not the author of confusion but of peace (1 Corinthians 14:33)" . This raid was a hostile array to strip and flay David and the people of Israel of their confidence during a time of transition. It was a gross expression of disrespect, unto David and his government. The Philistines were not seeking David to be friends but to defeat him. David desperately needed God's grace and guidance during this time of hostile attack so he humbled himself to seek God. At that time seeking God came through the priest but today we can go to our very own High Priest (Hebrews 4:14) Jesus Christ. Come to Jesus in humility of heart and soul and ask for direction and deliverance. David expressed this humility (Psalm 61), "From the ends of the earth I call to you, I call to you as my heart grows faint lead me to the rock that is higher than I." He acknowledges that he does not possess the strength or direction to get to God nor a place of safety without God's help-so he asks God to lead him. In a time of confusion and uncertainty David turned his attention toward God to get help because the heathen was raging. The Philistines share would be defeat because **God rewards humility with grace and pride with resistance**. I've taken this stance before and recall people calling me dumb or stupid because they wanted me to move out in my own power in a situation. I would wait to hear from God and then move. There is where I would find the blessing and never had to say a word because God would show that He was in control and not the individuals raging against me. People who operate in a spirit of control will always try to manipulate you to do what they want even when they don' t even have your best interest at heart they simply want to be in control because of what is lacking in their lives.

I am reminded of the praying tax collector in scripture he pictures humility so well. Scripture discloses this conversation from Luke 18:

"Two men went up to the temple to pray, one a Pharisee, the other a tax man. The Pharisee posed and prayed like this: 'Oh God, I thank you that I am not like other people-robbers, crooks, adulterers, or heaven forbid, like this tax man. I fast twice a week and tithe on all my income.' Meanwhile the tax man slumped in the shadows, his face in his hands, not daring to look up, said,

"God give me mercy. Forgive me a sinner." Jesus commented, "This tax man not the other went home made right with God. If you walk around with your nose in the air you' re going to end up flat on your face but if you' re content to be simply yourself you will become more than yourself."

Coming into true breakthrough will require acting in *active* faith instead of inflexible mindsets and familiar works. Flow with God and let God give you a strategy don' t get stuck in rituals. We are made right with God when we lean on and accept that it is His grace and mercy that opens the way for new and improved circumstances. Being humble does not mean your value as a person decreases however, it does infer your willingness to show a modest estimate of your importance in relation to God' s prevailing ability and preeminent position in the universe. In other words, stay humble, be obedient and move from the brink of a breakthrough to the plain evidence of breakthrough.

Empty sacrifices will get you nowhere in the kingdom of God but obedience to God always pays off! It is most times easier for us to do some vain sacrifice or to rattle off an "I did it" versus bring our minds, character and vows into obedience to God. Doing what we please over God' s commands calls for us to cleanse our hearts and our way. The prophet Samuel voiced this sentiment to King Saul so clearly when he stated (1 Samuel 15:22), "Has the Lord as great delight in burnt offerings and sacrifices, as in obeying the voice of the Lord? Behold to obey is better than sacrifice and to heed than the fat of rams." There is such a satisfaction and feeling of clear conscience when you obey what God has commanded you to do. It feels as though a path of blessing is open to you and that path is full of many different blessings along the way of life. Being obedient to God keeps us in a place of total dependence and surrender versus an incomplete sacrifice. God is a blessing God, it is his nature and he shows off his blessing nature in scripture to those who choose to obey his commands. He blesses mercifully and extravagantly to those who choose to walk in covenant with Him. So we can confidently say obedience pays out great dividends. The first dividend is having the sweet satisfaction of knowing that you have done the right thing because it is right not because there is a blessing attached to your obedience.

Relentless Passion

Keep pounding away, you are almost there, with all the effort you have put forth results are inevitable with the determination and effort you have placed on seeing your breakthrough. Now is time to be open to the fact that you are made for this breakthrough, made to go higher, to soar in life. It' s like the Word of God articulates so clearly for those who have been tired and on the brink, "but those who hope in the Lord will find new strength. They will soar high on wings like eagles. They will run and not grow weary, they will walk and not faint (Isaiah 40 NLT)." The word soar has been defined figuratively as ; to rise in thought, spirits or imagination-to be exalted in mood, don' t you think it' s time to soar? I believe your answer is yes, so take all the passion you have been using to stymie or even deadlock your success and let the molting process begin! God likens us to eagles for a reason they are strong and regal but even they go through a renewal process.

In 2 Samuel 5, David could have fainted when he heard giants were looking for him because of being God' s chosen. Have you ever been told someone was looking for you to fight you? Even if you knew you could take them it still incites fear because of the unknown. You' re all like, "why me I' m fabulous, everyone loves me." These giants were looking for David because he was anointed for service and the anointing attracts attacks! I bring this to light again it says of David, he went down to the stronghold. David says, "Light, space, zest! That' s God! So, with him on my side I' m fearless, afraid of no one and nothing." His confidence was in God not the giants so when he saw giants spread all over the valley just to defeat him but he did not let this attack contradict his being established as king! The enemy' s strategy is to scare you so bad that you run in fear without fortifying your life with the Word of God. He wants you paralysed in fear! The etymology of this word paralysed breaks down to beside and loosen or untie which is exactly the adversary' s plan to get beside us through situations and cause us to be untied or loosened from the word of God so he can use procrastination to destroy us and our purpose. The Valley of Rephaim was literally the Valley of giants. These giants not only displayed themselves but spread themselves out like a ball of dough being rolled out with a rolling pin for an extra-large pizza, you couldn' t miss them. Yet the king' s next action is paramount, he didn' t call his friends he called God and asked him, "What do you want me to do? Will I win this battle? Is it worth fighting?" And the Lord said, "Go get them, you will win, I' ve already gone before you. In essence, all David had to do was show up. The enemy spread out for David to beat him but God' s presence, broke out on the enemy! If in fact the annihilation was like water then it must have been a quick defeat; it is not many that come back from the current of rushing waters. David added action to his faith, scripture says, "So they came up to Baal-Perazim and David defeated them there." David was working together with God to defeat the giants. As it with our spiritual battles of faith we will win them by the power working in us as scripture states, "Now all glory to God, who is able through his mighty power at work in us to accomplish infinitely more than we ask or think. (Ephesians 3:20)."

God wants to give you a place of victory; he wants to give you a Baal-Perazim experience. God desires to give his people genuine breakthrough from the inside out. The force of God' s power in that valley was great, he is the Master of the breach; giving his people secret intelligence to help us attain the victory and to show the enemy who is truly in control. Get yourself in an advantageous position by enquiring of the Lord and trusting that Word. I keep going because God told me in a service once through the Apostle there, "The spirit of the Breaker anointing is on you!" So even when times get hard God reminds me I am with you, and like David I' ve anointed you for purpose not just for yourself but others as well, that' s double portion victory! When it was all said and done David gave God all the glory for the double victory he attained against the Philistines. We know after the first raid the Philistines attacked again and God gave David a stratagem to overthrow the enemy, the power of

God was with David as he fought. This teaches us that we should be in a constant "seek" for God. God never told us to ask for left over bread but daily bread. This happened with Abraham, God gave him an instruction to sacrifice Isaac, his only son to test the source of his worship and Abraham obeyed the word from God to sacrifice Isaac being his only son. Funny, right in the middle of his obedience to God came a fresh instruction from the Lord to stop the sacrifice and to get the ram in the bush for the sacrifice. God was never after his son, he wanted to know the reality of Abraham's faith was solely in Him as he does with us today. Wow, had Abraham not been in tune with the voice of God he would have missed the new, fresh instructions from God and missed God's provision. So in seeking your breakthrough stay in tune with God so he can show you where to glean and where to go and how to do what He is calling for. Stay in tune with God's timing. Don't make monuments out of your experiences with God, stay fluid he may want to bless you in a way you know not of for your present situation. It was by a sound

David won the battle so we must be in a place we can hear what God is relaying to us. David could have went on his accord but he did not he acknowledged God to get the right direction even though it was the same enemy. It behoves us to act on the Word of God when he gives it so we experience our jubilee from any form of bondage or debt to the enemy. Disobedience never pays in blessings only consequence. The Lord gave David a sudden advance of knowledge to thrash the Philistines. God' s strategies work. Jesus wants to restore us completely and give us overwhelming victories against our enemies so we may glorify Him alone.

This is a personal journey and our most striking tragedies; you know the ones that take your breath away? Those will be the events in our lives that bring us to the keenest introspection of ourselves and our lives. Its these experiences that have the potential to birth purpose. Personally, I had to say goodbye to procrastination, people-pleasing, pride and some other stuff but it had to go if I would truly move to the next dimensions that God already prepared for me. Further, I had to completely accept the call of God on my life and stop running because of what I might have to endure or be responsible for, I had to accept that God would be with me no matter what and that was all that mattered. **You see I believe if God is truly going to go before you and give you a grand breakthrough, you must come to the brink of yourself and be willing to confront any known behaviours that have kept you from being your authentic self.** In order to truly walk in the call of God you must know your God-identity first. You cannot function at your best personally or in relationships if you are not free to be who you truly are and that will cause grief. During a tough time in my marriage it seemed as though my husband and I couldn' t get on the same page if someone gave us the page number and gave explicit directions like, "bottom left dummies" , and I felt like I was giving all I had to try and succeed in our relationship. I was utterly exhausted, emotional and just downright sad most days. What was I to do and who was I to talk to? Most times in Christendom we are taught to profess victory over everything while dismissing the fact that we are emotionally and mentally drained as much as we confess the victory we do not have the victory. Reason being we are not taught to take care of ourselves, we are taught quick fixes and to just get over tough situations. Don' t get me wrong I am not advocating telling everyone your business but neither am I advocating sweeping situations under the carpet when they clearly need to be addressed and given the right prescription. What was left for me to do was get the Word of God on marital unity, act in love and allow the Holy Spirit to lead me through the situation. For example, I was made aware of a women' s conference during this time and that was part of my prescription, in addition I found a safe place to share my concerns so that I could be healed. Scripture advocates sharing our faults with each other and praying for each other so we can be healed (James 5:16). I got my focus off the situation and onto God and me then I experienced freedom more and more.

The Word of God and positive fellowship was my prescription for the time. During this time I needed to take it every day and when confused go back and take three times a day in double doses! Use the prescriptions that the Holy Spirit sends into your life because if you don' t you will remain sick, constantly confessing success and living a life void of victory. I was contemplating and praying about different avenues to take to alleviate the pain, distress and misunderstandings we had been having. Part of me just wanted out and part of me knew that the devil himself was attacking us because the devil knew if we were to be unified at this stage in our marriage we would do grave damage to his dark kingdom and propagate a legacy of successful marriage and family. So the enemy was doing everything he could to exasperate and exhaust us so that we would both give up on each other and our ministry. I was afraid of moving forward without my husband because we had been married so long and had already begun building legacy. You have to master the moment and ask yourself, "What do I need to do right now, which part of my prescription is needed right now to successfully navigate me through this moment, day, month, and year?

I felt like a failure because my career was not where I thought it should be at this point in my life, marriage was sour and ministry was transitioning a great deal. Surprised? Don' t be it happens to all of us and what we have to learn to do is not be ashamed of our struggles because ultimately God will use them for His glory. You see God is a redeeming God. Have you ever seen a coupon that says, "Redeem here" well; all those bad situations God says, "Redeem Here" for your good and His glory, now shout Hallelujah! So please do not be ashamed, shame is of the devil. God does not want you living in shame the devil does so let' s make that clear from the gate. Shame comes when we get acquainted with our sin and disobedience as in the Garden of Eden, "Then the eyes of both of them were opened and they suddenly felt shame at their nakedness so they sewed fig leaves together to cover themselves." You see God' s presence and shield was no longer covering them after they sinned so in their finite planning they tried to come up with a make-shift covering to cleanse themselves and remove their guilt. We still try to do that today but we do not have to struggle because Jesus Christ has forever redeemed us from the guilt and shame that sin brings upon us when we disobey God. In essence disobedience says to us, "Go ahead and sin, God is keeping stuff from you in the world" but obedience says, "No He isn' t and he is protecting me and blessing me right now." God' s will is the safest place for us, which is why the enemy tries so subtle yet persistent to persuade us from the will of God, in fact the safest place for believers. The devil wants you to think you are missing out but you must profess and trust, "God is enough for me!" Adam and Eve walked with God and they could trust Him but were duped into believing something else and ended up trusting a liar who promised enlightenment but only delivered darkness. True freedom requires coming clean with God and each other.

As we become more and more aware of our faults and shortcomings and *less and less* aware of our indwelling God-consciousness we walk in shame, guilt, pride and fear. On the flip side God can use the blush of shame we sometimes bear to bring us to a real encounter with Him, which in itself is breakthrough. Although I felt ashamed, I believed God used it to bring me to Him so I could take the medicine of His mercy and move on with life. I had all these negative questions, feelings of shame and thoughts evading my mind until the word of the Lord came to me, "We demolish arguments and every pretension that sets itself up against the knowledge of God and we take captive every thought to make it obedient to Christ." This knowledge was the first part of my breakthrough, I began to put this word into practice, every time a derogatory thought about anything came to my mind I took it captive and told that thought, "You will obey Christ, that negativity is not my inheritance" , and then I would speak the promise of God over myself out loud.

There were some things that had been set up against me from the enemy of my soul and he was counting on me to mirror my past and perpetuate a self-defeating cycle of thoughts that would keep me bound to a familiar cycle of setback and accept that as being ok. This is work and it is not easy but we can do it because the Holy Spirit is always present to help us in becoming more like Christ. Although I was in bitterness of soul, I knew I could not go on in this vicious cycle anymore; this breakthrough would take faith, obedience, courage and renewing my mind to see great transformation of me and my situation. God was revealing my inner turmoil as is indicated in James 4, "What causes fights and quarrels among you? Don' t they come from your desires that battle within you? You covet but you cannot get what you want, so you quarrel and fight. You do not have because you do not ask God. When you ask, you do not receive, because you ask with wrong motives, that you may spend what you get on your pleasures." It was a season of God ridding toxicity from my life and getting me to my authentic self which would lead to walking in true purpose. God sovereignly knew it was time for me to move forward in His perfect will and works for my life but He also knew I couldn' t do it with contamination. I needed to stop mirroring my circumstances let down my veil and cry it out before God, over and over! God will process you before he puts you in the palace.

Have you ever read the book of Psalms? King David noted sometimes as the sweet psalmist cried out to the Lord over and over with prayers, longings, confessions, and thanksgiving. In places of distress the Lord will look on you and respond to you which will take you out of the tight place and put you in large, broad space of liberty. In this place you learn to subtract your trust from the people, jobs etc even the most reliable ones that you have depended upon and set your trust in God alone. It is in this place you learn to be a giver and forsake stinginess and selfishness because you realize in giving out your life to Jesus in faith you get it back in fulfilment and blessing. It was a season of getting rid of barriers, false images and illusions in my life that could keep me from true blessing and purpose. **Just like in Judges 6, I would need to disavow the altars of previous**

generations, unhealthy habits and establish new altars of holiness and fidelity to the Lord.

I desperately needed to get beyond the barriers that I had placed on myself and my faith. I let others place barriers of ignorance in my life that defined me and God was not having that. Even though it would be painful I had to see the battle, embrace it and know he could breakthrough for me! The question I asked was, "Can I be this messed up and God still love me?" Yes, because even while we were enemies of God, He loved us; so how much more as his sons and daughters does he greatly love us now? My strategy would be to know and understand my true identity and inheritance in Jesus Christ. In addition, get in agreement with that blessing and throw out anything that was not a part of my godly inheritance. Knowing this I was able to give myself freedom to get little breakthroughs and big breakthroughs because, God planned all along for me to come forth in authenticity, operating in His power and in a real relationship with a real Saviour.

It' s time to get rid of the little wars inside that keep the limits on our life prosperity. God definitely wanted to show himself strong against the enemy of my identity and destiny as He does with all of His children.

We must know that what will affect us has the potential to infect us so learning to protect ourselves against spiritual viruses like erratic thinking or anger is essential. This process went on for months and even into the writing of this book.

As it happened I was in a training barely making it through a class having a deluge of thought, I called a good friend at a break and God used her to give me that *sudden advance of knowledge and an offensive thrust* that carried beyond the lines of the enemy' s warfare against me.

The spirit of the breaker was upon my mentor and friend to release an anointed Word in due time to move me beyond the gross deluge of thought and pain I was experiencing. Emotional pain can be the worst because it is unpredictable, you can be going along in a great mood and see something or someone and a trigger transports you to the pain. This is exactly why it can take a while for you to feel safe again but it is possible with the right support and of course the Word of God. Again, the reason I love the Psalms is because we all identify with the deep emotion penned by the writer, things like, "Lord how they have increased who trouble me! Many are they who rise up against me. Many who say of me, there is no help for him in God. But You Oh Lord are a shield for me; my glory and the One who lifts my head (Psalms 3)." God is the One who can ultimately lift our head, our thoughts and emotions out of trauma helping us to regulate our emotions and rebuild our ability to trust again. Certified therapy and support groups can help as well depending on your level of trauma or pain.

Back to the story, by the Spirit of the Lord that one conversation lifted me out of despair and into a place of refreshing, faith and hope. During that conversation the rivers of living water began to flow. Thank God for mentors, friends and leaders that get into the presence of God not only for them and take what they get from God and pour that oil of encouragement out on others. Encouragement that day came in tangible, practical things that I could do to walk in victory. As I was obedient to the instructions given to me I began to see results and gain a new confidence in God and myself.

That day I was offered these instructions, maybe they can help you to when you encounter an extremely difficult situation:

1. Focus on solutions not your problems.

2. Take more intentional time with God, worshipping Him, telling Him how much he means to you. Let God become the target of your attention (I took available moments in the car, at a coffee shop, walks to park, mailbox etc., to pray or read His Word, or short devotions that I could read and meditate on throughout my day. I also took time to get quiet and listened for God to speak to me.

3. In spending time around others remove yourself from negative comments or behaviours. Set emotional boundaries.

4. Speak positive affirmations daily over yourself, especially when you feel heavy or attacked.

5. Spend time doing things you like. Reward yourself.

6. Lastly she asked me a question, "Who is your source?" I answered, "God" Her reply, "Then you have got to trust God as Your Source for everything, not your job, husband, other relationships, but God alone. My expectation shifted and would continue to shift after this. I will also add to this, for us not to allow our surroundings and situations to reduce the power that comes from within, remain positive. Speak positive and as best you can do not let negativity get on the inside. You never need permission to be positive! This will be a

daily discipline but continue to pronounce that you are blessed, very good, great etc. in that you are changing your own atmosphere. You then put voice activated pressure on negative situations so they must align themselves with the Word of God that is in your mind and your mouth.

Time for WWE

After that conversation, I drove home that afternoon and again immediately put things into action along with taking every thought captive that was not lined up with the Word of God. Things looked as though they were getting worse and they sure felt that way. I had days after that, that were not so great but it did not take me as long to recover. Why? Because I truly believed what I was practicing and that I could do the things that I believed God placed in my heart to do even though they felt bigger than life. I believe a true vision from God will make you feel inadequate because he wants you to rely on tools to bring it to pass. We were created for prosperity and success and we will have to wrestle with life, like Jacob wrestled with God. Look at this from Genesis 32:

That night Jacob got up and took his two wives, his two female servants and his eleven sons and crossed the ford of the Jabbok. After he had sent them across the stream, he sent over all his possessions. So Jacob was left alone, and a man wrestled with him till daybreak. When the man saw that he could not overpower him, he touched the socket of Jacob's hip so that his hip was wrenched as he wrestled with the man. Then the man said, "Let me go, for it is daybreak." But Jacob replied, "I will not let you go unless you bless me. "The man asked him, "What is your name? "Jacob," he answered. Then the man said, "Your name will no longer be Jacob, but Israel, because you have struggled with God and with humans and have overcome. "Jacob said, "Please tell me your name. "But he replied, "Why do you ask my name?" Then he blessed him there. So Jacob called the place Peniel, saying, "It is because I saw God face to face, and yet my life was spared. "The sun rose above him as he passed Peniel, and he was limping because of his hip. Therefore to this day the Israelites do not eat the tendon attached to the socket of the hip, because the socket of Jacob's hip was touched near the tendon.

The brink of a breakthrough is a place of aloneness not loneliness. Being lonely is about missing people that make you feel like you belong to something and being alone is getting by yourself to get yourself together. There will many times in your walk with Christ that aloneness will come especially when God deems it is time for you to go to your next level. Each of these times God is trying to reveal more of Himself to you, which is your ultimate purpose, to know him more. Bordering breakthrough will be the place God can truly touch you as you send everything else you love spiritually into the hands of God and get alone with God. Some of us will be forced here, we will feel like Jacob, so sick of our situation and being taken advantage of that we abandon history and journey to encounter our God destiny.

Please don' t expect everyone to understand your journey because they won' t. Sometimes they will think you are being grandiose continue to love them and move forward, your life depends on you being committed to moving forward. Taking ultimate care and concern for you at this point will cultivate this same compassion and love for others. Frederick Buechner says this, "Jacob' s encounter at the Jabbok River is the magnificent defeat of the human soul at the hands of God." I can identify with this because I know what I like and how I want to live so therefore my soul needs to be subdued by the will of God that I may experience those types of blessings. God will not take you where your character won' t keep you. Here is where you admit your own character flaws and ask God for a changed name and new character. He will give it to you and speak to the direction your life will take. The place of grappling can become your biggest blessing because you can shed your culture and take on a kingdom culture. The brink of a breakthrough asks you to face fears and leave things and people behind that are not necessary for your personal life journey. The brink of a breakthrough can be scary but the Word of God admonishes us in Hebrews 12 to lay aside every weight and sin that so easily gets us off track in this life so we can run a successful race. There are times we feel like we are sacrificing the most important things and relationships, especially the ones we have become accustomed to but if they are not fulfilling and refining us they are most likely frustrating and depleting us.

The spirit of might will keep tapping you on the shoulder saying, "you can do this, let go, there is greater ahead." Courage will help lead you into the promises of God because breakthroughs are for risk takers not cowards. Sound strong, well I' m sorry but the road to good intention never led any one to success. Cutting negative or even relationships we deemed essential will carry some backlash with it but the spiritual yield of your obedience will far outweigh any potential repercussion of the enemy or people. The place of fighting with oneself is where you realize you cannot and will not go on without God! Even Jesus said, "You can do nothing without me (John 15:5). The place of tussling with God is where you choose transformation and kick conformity out of the window and say, "Goodbye!" We enter a place of being compelled to pray; for our intercession *is* our wrestling with God.

Being on the verge of lifestyle renovation is where you weep in request for the blessing of God and refuse the shame of failure, defeat and condemnation. You will not fail to get down on the wrestling mat so to speak and wrestle in prayer until God gives you a confirming yes in your spirit.

Here is where you stop caring about what people think and clench your commitment to a fulfilled life and better future. You will stand in the gap for your best life and everything connected to you. Your best life is in your spiritual inheritance from Jesus Christ. We are blessed when we depend solely upon God by living a life of faith. Faith blessed the patriarch Abraham and it still blesses us today, "So those then who live by faith are blessed with faithful Abraham-who lived by faith, this is no new doctrine (Galatians 3 MSG). So it is up to us to ask for it and appropriate the blessing in our lives by faith.

Intercession is pleading with God on behalf of your needs and the needs of others. The fierce place of intercession; standing in the gap is where your tenacity shows up to plead the mercy of God Here you are armed with the knowledge that you have Jesus Christ backing you assuring you that you will hit life' s bulls eye and experience the momentum of breakthrough to the destination of answered prayer. After leaving intercessory prayer (time and again) you will have a "knowing" that all is well and a confidence that whatever was opposing you has now lost the battle. Sometimes we won' t even have the words yet the Holy Spirit can help us to pray and helps our infirmities and intercedes for us without words yet with costly cries and expensive groans (Romans 8:26). Intercession is where your need and God' s knowledge and power intersect. Intercession is where Jesus intervenes in life' s situations for you with His victory over death, hell, the grave and the law.

The Great High Priest intercedes on our behalf like it says in Romans 8, "Who then is the one who condemns? No one. Christ Jesus who died-more than that, who was raised to life – is at the right hand of God interceding for us." No one else has the merit, the badge of honour, excellence or assets to stand in our stead and appropriate the will of God for our lives except Jesus Christ. His sacrifice, death, burial, resurrection and ascension alone more than qualify Him to arbitrate on our behalf against every accuser including ourselves. Jesus is in the presence of God interceding on our behalf, not proving a case because He already won the case on our behalf. Everything His death accomplished, (all benefits) He is interceding to apply them to our account because we are joint heirs with Him. His intercession is constant as His love is vehemently and constantly coming after us. He is listening for our prayers and declaring them as His will, declaring blessing upon us and seeing that the benefits of His death are applied to us by His design. This spiritual place is where you take hold of God and God takes hold of you, you are not alone. This place of prayer pressure is where "no" is not an option; your life depends on God's yes. And His promises to us are always yes and amen (2 Corinthians 1:20). When you prevail in prayer you prevail against the enemy. Your solitude may hurt but it is valuable, the place of quietness and crying out to God is valuable. The birth pangs of life are actually enlarging you to full deliverance not diminishing you as the enemy and life would make you feel.

Brawling with God is where we struggle with God in our humanity to leave behind all the known, prevalent behaviours that have plagued us for a lifetime. Like Jacobs life beginning at birth

(Genesis 25:26) he continued to grab for things attained by his flesh and by his power, just like us today. I truly relate to Jacob in that throughout my life I have been called the runt of the litter which made me grab for what I could and be satisfied. Jacobs name means supplanter or heel-grabber which signifies the behaviours believer' s grapple with today; to be so in control that we will do it at the cost of others and even self-sabotage our true life, a life led and fuelled by the Spirit of God. Oh how many times have I sabotaged my Spirit life because I was afraid and conformed to what looked like a blessed life? Many times I conformed but was not blessed by God at all because neither my mind nor my actions were renewed by the Word of God completely. I needed deliverance from myself because I wanted to do well but something else was working in me to keep interrupting my full blessing. It' s likened unto Paul when he says, "So I find this law at work: all though I want to do good evil is right there with me (Romans 7:21). It' s like being in the movie Ground Hog Day where the main character, a weather man finds himself living the same day over and over again, that day was Ground Hog Day.

The character is frustrated about covering a story and he shows his frustration openly. He uses his foreknowledge to his advantage at first until he realizes that he is doomed to doing the same things each and every day. He was exiled to this same day as a life lesson to see who he actually is, which is not so great of a person. Many situations mostly bad lead him to the knowledge of his authentic self. Thank God we are not condemned to this evil; we can live above sin by the power of Christ working in us and through us. So we too feel stuck until a greater force comes along and moves us into the blessing of our authentic selves to live a true life and serve others.

Real faith requires walking in "real time" with hope to actually see what you believe to come to pass. Genuine faith is never immobile but always active, always expecting manifestation for what you are pursuing in prayer.

I was walking in fake, not faith and I can say that because as I look back I was taken care of by God but I was not walking in total freedom that obedience and total dependence on God brings to our lives. Don' t get cocky because each of us has a little of Jacob in us and we are trying to get to the place where God changes our name and gives us a new beginning. We know that His nature is consistent with new beginnings because the Word tells us what He says, "Behold I will do a new thing, now it shall spring forth. Shall you not know it? I will make a road in the wilderness and rivers in the desert (Isaiah 43:19). God' s nature loves and He is committed to new beginnings for those that have lost their way.

We grab things that look like success because we are used to conforming to the world instead of allowing the Spirit of God to transform us to the likeness of Jesus which would produce His blessings. Mostly because we want what we want right now! What have you grabbed lately that you need to put down because it was produced by the flesh?

The brink is where you and God are in a night season, here is where you are crying out to God, "You said and your word says!" This place is where God fights with you and tests your tenacity so you won' t give up. He wants you to see that you can do it. He' s showing you how to keep applying your faith which is the economy of heaven in which He himself cannot deny! Here is where you cry tears all the way to work, mess up your make up, pull over and put it back on again. On your journey the most important thing now is crying out to God in prayer as He wrestles with you. Keep it up, just like Jacob resolve to grapple with God until you see change and see a difference in you and your circumstances. As you do this a new tenacity shows up in you that will be determined to win and finish what you started. This wonderful place is where we face the fact that life is not easy but it is also the place where we receive God' s blessing. At this point we' ve given up much but realizing its time to live life to full will be well worth the fight. God could have easily overcome Jacob but instead he encouraged his faith, God loves mercy over judgment. Jacobs' s victory was not by His own hand but by one

Superior to Him and yet God was showing Jacob that he very well could come to a place of truth, authenticity and victory.

The blessing of breakthrough comes after rolling around on the ground kicking up dust with God concerning your life. Ask yourself, will I stop being lazy and get the blessing? He wants to know if you really want this, if you will truly give all away that is near and dear to you (not that He needs it) but just to know that you are making yourself available to Him without reservation. When we do this, we look like God' s image because he gave his prized possession to us. Jesus touched the hollow of Jacobs hip during the wrestling match and dislocated his hip to remind Jacob that the very things that he was now to hang up and alienate things that held his life captive and contrary to blessing. This touch was a reminder that my life is out of joint without the One who created me.

This is the place where life touches you with a painfully beneficial touch to leave you with a sign that God is severing you from negative soul ties, barren behaviours, fear of abandonment, fear of people, and fear of success and being uncreative. This touch would remind Jacob of his disgust with himself and his need of total dependence on God. For us it is the death of our independent, carnal self-life to the real, authentic life God created for us before the foundations of the world. This new way of life will be a journey but it starts with the touch of brokenness encountered by wresting in prayer with God. The threshold of advancement is where we are disabled to be enabled by God for the life He chose in Christ for us to live by His Spirit!

After the touch, the Angel said, "Let me go for the dawn is breaking" and Jacob who had used his grabbing for bad finally used it to grab and ask the right person to bless him. He finally used his "gift for grab" if you will, to ask Jesus for his life-blessing instead of asking everyone else. Then Jesus asked him a simple question, "What is your name?" and in essence he was asking Jacob who he truly was and Jacob gave the only answer he was capable of giving, "Jacob, a conniver, a heel-grabber, a trickster and a schemer" he was honest with God and himself in that crucial moment. When we are absolutely honest with God we realize how small we are and how big God is and that He is enough.

The One with the true power, Jesus Christ gave him a new name at the break of day, that name was Israel. The Hebrew word for Israel connotes to strive with God and comes from the words el and Sarah meaning to rule as God. This makes perfect sense because Jacob as do we need to walk and rule in the earth as ambassadors of Christ who hear him, obey him and act like him in the absence of His person. In addition, the name means prince foreshadowing our Prince of Peace, (Isaiah 9:6) Jesus Christ. A prince does only what the king dictates, Jesus is the perfect example of how to follow God. Jesus says, "Very truly I tell you, the Son can do nothing by Himself; he can do only what he sees his Father doing, because whatever the Father does the Son also does (John 5:19)." So we are to model ourselves today to live by the examples of Christ to look and act like our

Father in Heaven. It's possible! We are made in the image and likeness of God and His image in us should be as close a resemblance as a shadow. Just like you cannot be separated from your shadow, neither should we be able to separate our characteristics from Gods', we should in essence look like Him in deed and action. He even tells us in Matthew 5:48 "In a word, what I'm saying is grow up. You're kingdom subjects. Now live like it. Live out your God-created identity. Live generously and graciously towards others, the way God lives toward you." Your Jesus perfectly resembled the Father in his time spent on Earth that is why he was able to say to the disciples, "If you really know me, you will know my Father as well. From now on, you do know him and have seen him (John 14:7). He was saying if you want to know the Father look at me, look at how I walk, talk, act and react then you will have seen the Father. Jesus was the spitting image of His Father. There will come a time when the Jacob in us will get tired of the night seasons and yet continue to fight but it takes God to call it and say enough is enough, let's get real, "Who are you?"

Seasons Change

Pay attention when God starts asking you questions He is revealing something to you and releasing something to you as well, blessing or not will be up to you. Keep wrestling until God says to you, it's almost daybreak! The word could come in a sermon, your quiet time, or a prophetic message like it did for me. I knew my seasons were changing when during a prayer meeting a pastor released the Word of the Lord to me saying, "The last three years of your life have been a time of refining. These years have created intimacy between you and the Father. You are seasoned, tried and proven.

Yes, you have been misunderstood but you will be vindicated and I have seen your sacrifice. I am directing you into favour and connections. I am giving you supernatural strength and I am going to strengthen your ministry. Get ready for platform for I am already stirring this. I will speak business ideas to ministry to the next level. In six months your life won't look the same. The breaker anointing is on you." By this I knew all the trouble, hard times and misunderstandings were tools in the Vinedresser's hand to prune me for purpose. God's Word to me that evening spoke to me at my core, just like Jacob and I knew I would never be the same. God had spoken his blessing over me and I had to stay connected at this level of breakthrough. Jesus said, "I am the vine, you are the branches. When you' re joined in me and I with you, the relation intimate and organic, the harvest is sure to be abundant. Separated you can' t produce a thing. Anyone who separates from me is deadwood, gathered up and thrown on the bonfire. But if you make yourselves at home with me and my words are at home in you, you can be sure that whatever you ask will be listened to and acted upon. This is how my Father shows who he is-when you produce grapes, when you mature as my disciples (John 15:5-8 Message).

At the point of breakthrough you are you the branch are allowing the life of Christ to flow through you instead of striving by works like I talked about in the beginning. Abiding in the vine and producing fruit is you bringing heaven to earth. This gives our heavenly father joy.

Daybreak announces light, newness, courage, restoration, breakthrough and good changes. The blessing comes at daybreak! No matter how long and gruelling our night season will come to an end and we will see our due season and bear fruit! How do I know that because the Angel announces to Jacob the dawn is here, its morning and you made it through the night. The morning is an indication of transformation and sure change in our situations. Scripture proves this to us when it says, "Weeping may endure for a night but joy comes in the morning (Psalm 30:5)meaning that which we weep for has only a season to allow us to grieve healthy and the learning of lessons but then revival and life will come again. In my experience every time we bring our broken hearts and tears before the Father there is a supernatural exchange. When we have the courage to cry it out before Him this very experience scours our hearts a little a time producing a releasing of weight and a cleansing of soul. It's like scripture says, "Those who go out weeping, carrying seed to sow, will return with songs of joy, carrying sheaves with them. By sowing the Word into our minds and hearts in the season of pain we assured a harvest of joy! Your labour of faith will not go unrewarded. You are sowing into the good ground of yourself, your life, your purpose.

God pronounced this place a place of breakthrough and victory in the spiritual realm and the natural realm. Your name will no longer be Jacob, but Israel, because you have struggled with God and with humans and have overcome." Jesus says to Jacob, your name is Israel, for as a prince you have power with God and with men and have prevailed. So it is with us God uses our encounters with Him to change our character to resemble his.

Power belongs to God (Psalm 62:11) and emanates from God so he can issue His power as he pleases. God gave Jacob power to prevail in faith through the night to show Jacob his true character, the character of prince will contend and persist until he prevails. In studying princes I found that a prince undertakes great projects and gives striking proofs of his capacity, he is a great friend or a through foe; he is never neutral and admonishes others to never be neutral but to choose their side. A prince honours those of every art and encourages people to pursue their calling as to enhance the kingdom.

A good prince maintains the dignity of his office yet also entertains the people and shows interest in society (bartleby.com). I do not believe God would have called Jacob a prince if he was not going to empower him to act like a prince of God. As it is today, what God calls us to do he equips and empowers us to carry out the assignment to completion. God perfects the things that concern us (Psalm 138:8) which means the things that we set out to do by faith according to His will He will cause us to complete. He will give us the power to complete what He started in us even if it feels a little shaky at times. God is amazing in that he shows us who we truly are through times of struggle. So although the fight through the night can make us very uncomfortable and cause us to question God at times He promises to complete the work. He started a good work in us and will bless us with the resources needed to accomplish his purpose in the Earth.

So if you are sitting here today wondering, "How am I going to get unstuck?" you are already on your way by reading and applying the principles you have learned in this short book. Prioritize you, renewing your mind and your purpose! Remember trusting God for your breakthrough will require foregoing your own understanding, your culture and taking on the mind of God concerning you and your situations. Faith never denies reality, yet when used effectively can change us and our state of affairs. Near the end of finishing this book, I had a day full of miscommunications and disappointments, it was horrible. I didn' t get paid for clients I' d serviced, my group facilitator failed to tell us our class was cancelled, my daughter' s playdate was cancelled due to lack of preparation, and I needed car repairs and so much more. At the end of that day, I took a deep breath, shed a few tears as I sat in my car and began thanking God and reminding Him of His promise to me. As I drove away I felt the heaviness of the day begin to lift. I used the Word as weapon to cut down the potential heaviness ready to pounce on me. All that was left to do was prioritize my responsibilities, execute them where necessary and continue on my journey. Taking a breather will be important, after days like that, go take care of you. Believe me the problems will still be there to be solved.

Getting unstuck will require us to stop letting our environment dictate defeat to us. Now is time to allow health from the Word of God to put us "in the pink" meaning in very good health, condition physically and emotionally (freedictionary.com). Change and growth are inevitable so we must be apt and equipped to handle them when they come so that we do not get stuck on the merry-go-round of life. Be humble before God so that you can get the answers you need to proceed into breakthrough. Scripture says clearly, that God favours the humble (James 4:6) and resists the proud so if you are going to obtain a breakthrough you must walk lightly before God, but be honest with Him he can handle it. God knows what you are thinking and even the next words you are going to speak, His grace is sufficient for you (2 Corinthians 12:9) and every situation you will encounter.

The word grace here means that God is freely extending Himself, reaching out to people because He is disposed to bless them and be near them. Wow, isn' t that amazing? That God loves us so much he is always leaning in to make sure we encounter Him and receive His many benefits. Those benefits can be all types of blessing like direction, soul-healing, a miracle, financial breakthrough, mentorship, a word of wisdom, and so much more. What you are going through is more about who you are becoming that what you are doing or going to do. What you are going to do will be evident when Gods character becomes more and more evident in you.

Get it back

You are God' s champion, period. So all of the other voices telling you different from what the Word of God is speaking to you, those voices are lying to you. It's time to get your value, vision and voice back! You are not just a conqueror but you are more than a conqueror. Believe that, because what you believe will determine how you act from here. God wants to accelerate you into purpose; the enemy only wants to reduce you to your past and fear of your future. Where ever you are in your quest for purpose work with excellence like you're already there. The more responsibility you take for where you are the more power you take back over your life. Pray about major decisions and ask God for his direction. When you believe you've heard God give you assignments continue to bathe it in prayer until you get a sure release to move on it. The worse thing we can do is hear God but move outside of his timing for us. Let's recap a little, remember to get a clear vision for your life by asking some serious reflective questions like these;

1. Why am I stuck personally, relationally or professionally?

2. What am I passionate about? What do you gravitate naturally toward?

3. What do I dream about doing?

4. Where do I want to go from here?

5. What do I need to get there?

6. What does the word of God say about it?

7. Am I on the right frequency to hear God?

8. Your relationship with God is important so make it a highlight in your life.

9. Study where you want to go. Google it!

10. Do something small everyday toward your goal. Prioritize your purpose.

You may think of more questions/statements than these, but I think this will get your thinking juices flowing and give you some prayer points. Also remember that the forces against your success are real, they are both spiritual and natural. Arm yourself with the Word of God and prayer. Get around other purpose minded people.

When I truly began to hone my purpose I took a class about it to truly get clear on my assignment. It is when you come to end of yourself that God can truly begin to show up. God helps his people when all other helps fail and they feel they are sinking and then he teaches their hands to wage war. David says, "Praise be to the Lord, who trains my hands for war and my fingers for battle (Psalm 144:1)." God will teach you how to handle the sword, which is the Word of God. A prophetess once told me, "No matter what happens, don' t stop speaking the Word of God. Feed on the Word, and no matter how you feel don' t stop speaking the Word of God." She admonished me, "Even if you mess up and speak something negative during the time of your breakthrough, repent, cancel the words out in Jesus Name and speak the word only." Even the Lord Himself is a man of war (Exodus 15:3) and so he will teach us the art of spiritual warfare to be strong in Him and the power of His might. God wants to display his power through his Word, through the Gospel of

Jesus Christ. He gives us spiritual armour (Ephesians 6:10-18), shows us how to wear the armour, and how to use the armour to stand and defeat our spiritual enemies. Put it on prayerfully each and every day! Identify the forces arrayed against you, pray about them and know Jesus said in Luke 10:19, "I have given you authority to trample on snakes and scorpions and to overcome all the power of the enemy; nothing will harm you." You are fighting from a place of victory in Christ Jesus. Yes the devil is real but he is also defeated by Christ Jesus works on Calvary. During your prayer time be led by and open to the Spirit remember you don' t need more works that make you feel like you are failing just do the work He is giving you to do.

Remember God gave David different strategies to defeat the enemy and he will give us strategies too. In one battle David was to charge the battle with force and in another he was to wait to hear a specific sound (which was a sign to move forward) from above in the trees before he struck the Philistines all the way back to the borders of their own country. Today that could be likened unto God giving you a word of wisdom (a gift of the Holy Spirit) for a specific situation. A word of wisdom from someone gifted with this endowment throws light on a situation helping us to apply the spoken word of knowledge at just the right time in a situation. Even the New Testament apostles were to wait in the upper room. Keep in mind our battle will not be won by might, nor by power but by the Spirit of the Lord (Zechariah 4:6) we will win every battle. Lastly, remember what you have learned in each battle, it will benefit you and others in the future.

We learned earlier to undertake a serious paradigm shift, basically to come into agreement with what God says and what he says about you as your new truth. It is the truth of God that makes you free and God wants you free from any form of bondage; past, present and even future. God wants you to prosper in every area of your life. God wants you to have soul prosperity which comes from the Word of God and prayer. Take on an attitude of prayer and worship. Pray consistently and fervently to fellowship with God and to see breakthrough in every area of your life. Let me say don' t make your prayer life ritualistic, pray anywhere all the time and listen to what God is say to you as well. We recall that the effectual, fervent, prayer of the righteous man avails much (James 5:16).

Our prayers should be full of energy and life. By the Holy Ghost your energetic prayers bring the situation from one stage to the next like an electrical current that energizes a wire which brings it to a shining light bulb that lights a room. God is trying to get His will in the earth through you, so stay in touch with God! Ask according to God' s will and he will put the right desires and dreams within your heart. The Holy Spirit will put the right inbirthings in your spirit so you pray the persuasion of God' s will over yours. Your passionate, intentional prayers will work for you and others. God wants you to win this battle so you are assigned appropriately to your purpose in His perfect timing. Let God show you what He has been dreaming about for your life. Trust God with your future and the season you are currently wading through.

There is a set time for you to come out of testing in triumph! I spent months crying and confessing and still do a little bit of both but I am convinced we are in a time that God is going to cause us to reap in joy. God' s heart is good towards us and his thoughts toward us are good, He calls us very good and has planned a good future for us. Press through the pain into purpose with the assurance that you will laugh and dance again. No matter what you are going through God' s grace is sufficient for you. What does that mean; it means God' s kindness is always reaching out to help you through each and every situation you encounter. Though the situation is nagging you, though the enemy is buffeting you, Gods kindness and blessing through the situation will always outweigh the tribulation. So do not allow the situation to cause you to shrink in faith or Christ like identity.

You are not a grasshopper, even if the enemy is trying to make you feel like one. This journey you' ve been on has literally been a journey to the real you. I'm speaking of the regenerated person you become after accepting Jesus Christ as your Lord and Saviour, the "you" that is made in the image and likeness of God and constantly being transformed to be like Christ through the power of the Holy Spirit. Grass hopper mentality says, "I am small in my own eyes and other people think I am nothing too" it is also concerned with what other people look like and what they are doing. This mentality is contagious to affect others in a negative way and cause them to look back forfeiting what God has already freely given.

Having a grasshopper spirit will make you a complainer instead of a dreamer. Careful what you allow into your ears. A great help to me while I was on the brink of a breakthrough was listening to sermons on line, music or other means to feed my spirit causing me to have a "can do" attitude. In order to experience breakthrough you will need to have a can do attitude, like scripture says, "You can do all things through Christ who strengthens you (Philippians 4:13). You will also have to be around people that have a "can do "faith-filled attitude to propel you into what God has for you. Be around those that don' t mind confessing their weaknesses and depending solely upon God in faith to see the good land he has prepared for the taking. You have got to know the vision that God has given you for your life is good and is far better than what you have planned. God' s plans for you will yield the success and satisfaction that you so long for, so decree and declare, "What God has planned for me is good." It benefits us to have a good view of God, sometimes we equate God with man and this is not right. Sometimes we equate the unfair, upsetting, wounding and painful experiences that we have had with man and put them to God' s account when he is not like man. Man' s love is conditional and God' s love for us is unconditional and he wants to see us breakthrough to the next dimension of purpose and prosperity.

Breakthrough by definition is an act of overcoming or penetrating an obstacle, restriction or a military offensive that penetrates an enemy' s line of defence; a significant or sudden advance, development etc. as in scientific knowledge (freedictionary.com). So we can safely say that breakthrough causes us to have productive insight, important discovery and the penetration of an enemy's barriers in our lives. A true breakthrough is our realizing who God is and who we are. Before breakthrough comes there will be a sure time of testing; a testing of faith and the word working in our lives. Will we have the faith to speak and obey the Word of God for a specific situation? This is the question that will be posed to us as we perch the brink of a breakthrough.

These very acts of testing are overcoming the lies we have believed about God, ourselves and our situations. The brink of a breakthrough requires courage to press in and get rid of the lie that stagnation is our portion. It may seem a little wild and crazy for a time but be assured God is a God of order and is working to bring order to your life through these tests. When we allow God to revolutionize our thinking, actions and reactions God can create divine appointments of destiny for us. Although the enemy may be arrayed against us in a great way our perspective and response to test and trial will determine our breakthrough. I'd like to admonish you to praise God for coming to the brink of a breakthrough. Your praise will work for you causing you to emerge beyond enemy lines, bringing confusion to his camp and victory to your life. God not only wants you to win but to plunder the enemy and get all of his images out of your life. The word commands us to worship the Lord God only.

Remember the angel of the Lord gave Gideon in Judges 6 a strategy for the nation to come back into alignment with God because they were being defeated by the Midianite enemy. Gideon was instructed to tear down the altars of Baal and build a new altar unto God. In building these new principles in your life you will be persecuted as Gideon was the men said to him, "Who has done this thing?" The enemy and even people will have the audacity to tell you, "It doesn't take all that to be a Christian!" But the devil is a liar, God wants to give you a new view and that's a kingdom view and perspective.

The enemy does not want you to think, he wants you to beg and wade in stagnation. Go forward in God supplied with the promises of God! Even though the enemy was persecuting Gideon he was protected. The Prophet Joash stood to declare, " "Would you plead for Baal? Would you save him? Let the one who would plead for him be put to death by morning! If he *is* a god, let him plead for himself, because his altar has been torn down!" Stick to your guns because when you are on assignment for God he has got your back! Be confident of this that the same God who broke through David' s enemies can break through our enemies today! How can you say that? I can because God does not change, His word does not change, he says of himself, "I change not" and he is the same yesterday, today and forever. His methods may change but He nor His Word will change, it is settled so expect to see the glory of God.

We as believers will experience tribulation but that tribulation definitely has a return on investment for our lives; it will yield the revenue of perseverance. Perseverance is steadfastness in doing something despite difficulty or delay in achieving success (google search). Those who put forward a little more energy will experience breakthrough. I know some days we want to throw perseverance out the window and jump ship but that determination and grit are the foundation of our character to handle the places God wants to take us for the kingdom's sake. We are armed with the knowledge that no matter what we go through it will work out for our good because we love God and are called according to His purpose. It may not feel good or look good but will work together for your good (Romans 8:28).

At the brink of your breakthrough your godly character will develop and emerge and new hope will emerge for the present and the future. Walking out the testing of our faith with God produces an expectation of what is sure (God's promises) and in this new anticipation for breakthrough we are not disappointed. But rather have come to an appointment with God for purpose in this lifetime. I believe part of my breakthrough was to finish the assignment of writing this book and I am just about done. God desires to use your story for His glory. Will you work together with God to advance the cause of Christ to see souls saved, delivered, healed and set free? Your purpose is bigger than your immediate circle or circumstances. The force of God on your side is more than the world against you and you have to believe that to experience breakthrough. Know that every season has a reason, get to the reason, pass the test and move to the next level in your life. Move your thinking from the place of what you can do and what you have to line up with what He can do by His miraculous power. Put what little strength you have left put into God' s hands, let him bless it and break it as Jesus did in John 6. Let Jesus the Breaker go to work in your situation by extending your faith in God' s Word and power. We can still use our faith to see miracles.

Belief in God' s timing, provision and pre-determined will for your life must become more important than your next place. Do what is important first for every area of your life be it spiritually, relationally, financially etc. by the leading of the Holy Spirit. Ask God for His leading on the matter and He will because He promised to by saying, "The Lord directs the steps of the godly, he delights in every detail of their lives (Psalm 37:23). Even the smallest of details your Heavenly Father is excited to get involved with concerning our lives? Isn' t that wonderful? Do not forfeit the lessons of the journey or you will forfeit the ultimate time for your gifts to make room for you.

Embrace your transition and let God stretch you so he can fill you for what is next. When I started asking the question, "What am I supposed to be learning God?" it revolutionized my life because I was not so bent toward performing to get results. I was taking time to walk and talk with the One who delighted in my life and transforming before my own eyes. Does God want you to have results and success? Absolutely, God wants you to have success but not at the expense of losing your closeness with him and deepening your relationship with Him. I believe we pointed out earlier that eternal life is not just going to heaven but knowing God. Will you allow God to bring about a greater weight of glory in your life? Meaning will you allow the emptying of yourself, the unpacking of the effects of the past in order for God to transform you into the key kingdom player he birthed you into Earth realm to be? Again, your pain may parallel your progress but don' t give up use the friction to quicken you into the grace to get to the next dimension of assignment.

When we come to the brink of breakthrough we have come to a great place to partner with God. This place of partnership allows God to renovate barren places in our lives. People will ask you to stay little so they are comfortable but refuse this tactic of quack and lack. That means you are like an eagle made to fly high and soar at certain levels but people who enjoy low level living just want to keep you talking bad (quacking) and living bad (lacking). God does not want you to just survive but to thrive in life. We can go from barren to fruitful by the power of God to experience a sudden advance and significant change in our desperate situations.

A breakthrough is God speaking good over us, a benediction (bene, meaning good and diction meaning word) over us so we will take and use that word to advance our lives past the border of the enemy into a new, fresh place in God. Your situation may look pathetic but look to the prophetic word God has spoken over you. God will perform his promise and give us the grace to breakthrough, take it! Whatever is not of God in your life will fall and only what you do for Christ will last. This whole process is for us to grow in confidence, dependence and providence towards God.

You are a winner, keep fighting and see what the end will be, you have the Ultimate Helper for every battle. Walk in your true identity in Christ as a believer not a beggar. Once the environment on the inside begins to change it is inevitable that your outside circumstances begin to change. If you begin to mirror the God-image you are called to your circumstances will inevitably get there. Use this time on the brink of a breakthrough to give you the thrust you need to take off into different realms like a rocket. You will see ordained victory in this realm and the next the scripture confirms that by saying, "Then the seventh angel blew his trumpet, and there were loud voices in heaven, saying, "The kingdom of the world has become the kingdom of our Lord and of his Christ, and he shall reign forever and ever (Revelation 11:15)."

When you win (not if) remember to give God glory. When God goes before your enemies breaking out upon them like a breakthrough of water, give God praise for using you in the matter to see what is really working on the inside of you. God can and will drown the enemies that have been trying to drown you.

God wants you to know what you are working with so that the next time you come to a brink you recall the God of the breakthrough. Know this, your trials are for preparation and your final destination is victory. Breakthrough will require sacrifice, obedience, faith, courage, humility, fierce determination and even some tears. Breakthrough will acquire a deeper walk with God, new trust in Him, godly character, boldness for living, new momentum, gifts, rewards, miracles, favor, victory over your enemies and divine appointments.

In God we live, move and have our being and we are his offspring (Acts 17:28). He gladly owns us as his offspring and has lavishly provided for us, even through the fiercest trials of life. Remember you are not a grasshopper! Let winning your small battles spur you on to win great victories in life. Remember to set your mind on things above and free your mind of thoughts that restrict you to being or feeling stuck in a certain place.

Free yourself from the belief that you are responsible to nurse and judge every thought that comes to mind. What should free us is the fact that God is our final judge, because he always judges right. Take comfort in the fact that it is not our job to judge or justify our past, people we know and/ or even ourselves. The Word of God is our best leader when proving our justification and total wellness. Even the Apostle Paul said, "But to me it is a very small thing that I may be examined by you or by any human court, in fact I do not even examine myself. For I am conscious of nothing against myself, yet I am not by this acquitted but *the one who examines me is the Lord.*" Let the Lord examine you, in your time of meditation and quiet, let God speak to you about you. God takes the foolish things of this world to confound the wise and He takes the weak things of the world to shame the strong so do not be ashamed of your journey. You can stop vacillating between being down in the dumps and dancing into destiny by acknowledging God as your ultimate source and pointing your passion toward true purpose. Clear your mind of "I can' t" and look into the mirror of God' s Word and finally see yourself as you truly are, valuable. You are a masterpiece created for good works. It is always best to know who you truly are before you do what you are called to do. Why? You want to your character kinks worked out before you take your platform whether it is public speaking, owning a restaurant or teaching in a classroom. Don' t downplay the process; embrace it because you gain invaluable resources in your "valley" experiences that will qualify you for your mountain tops. Remember it' s a journey not a destination and no matter how small your steps just let your direction be forward. I cannot stress enough holding dear the Word of God, whether it is your private study, at church, or a prophetic word spoken to you it will help you transition as you go from faith to faith. It will give you victory and ground to stand on when at times it seems all else if failing. Know this, little is much when God is involved so live, look up and get up; the time for your breakthrough is now!

If you enjoyed any part of this Breakthrough Manifesto, go to Amazon.com and leave a review. Be blessed,

Kimberly

References:

Environmental Division-Vehicle Facts and Myths. http://www.chesterfield.gov/content2.aspx?id=16660

Frederick Buechner, "The Magnificent Defeat" P. 18.

http://m.frederickbuechner.com/content/magnificent-defeat-page-18

Harvard Classics-Volume 36 Part 1 Number 21, "The Prince". http://www.bartleby.com/36/1/

Portia Nelson, "There' s a whole in my sidewalk." The Romance of Self Discovery.

http://www.goodreads.com/quotes/95085-i-walk-down-the-street-there-is-a-deep-hole

http://www.biblegateway.com/

For any reference to Greek/Hebrew words or translation; http://biblehub.com/

Contact the Author:

Kimberly Lee

B2bcoachkim@gmail.com

http://Breakthroughnow.wix.com/breakthrough now